FED WATCHING AND INTEREST RATE PROJECTIONS

A Practical Guide

David M. Jones
Senior Vice President and Economist
Aubrey G. Lanston & Co., Inc.

New York Institute of Finance

Library of Congress Cataloging-in-Publication Data
  Jones, David M. (David Milton)
    Fed watching and interest rate projections.

    Bibliography: P.
    Includes index.
    1. Board of Governors of the Federal Reserve
System (U.S.) 2. Interest rates--United States.
I. Title.
HG2563.J66   1986   332.1'13'0973   86-8433
ISBN 0-13-308313-6
ISBN 0-13-308321-7 (pbk.)

This publication is designed to provide accurate and authoritative information in regard to the subject matter covered. It is sold with the understanding that the publisher is not engaged in rendering legal, accounting, or other professional service. If legal advice or other expert assistance is required, the services of a competent professional person should be sought.

—*From a Declaration of Principles jointly adopted by a Committee of the American Bar Association and a committee of Publishers and Associations*

Printed in the United States of America

10   9   8   7   6   5   4   3   2   1

New York Institute of Finance
(NYIF Corp.)
70 Pine St.
New York, New York 10270

This book is dedicated to my parents, who made everything possible; and to my wife Becky and children—David, Jennifer, and Stephen—who make it all worthwhile.

Contents

Appendixes, 137

Charts

Tables

*P*reface

There have been many systems calculated to make a killing in the bond and stock markets. Some identify purely technical buy or sell signals, some are based on complicated wave theories, and some make use of fundamental economic and financial analysis. But the key to successful investing in the bond and stock markets can be as simple as being adept at anticipating policy shifts by the Federal Reserve (Fed).

The monetary authorities react to undesired swings in economic activity and monetary growth by shifting policy to tighten or ease bank reserve pressures. A mere change in investor expectations concerning these Fed policy shifts—quite apart from the reality of the shifts themselves—can powerfully influence interest rate movements.

So, what is Fed watching all about? It involves knowing how Fed policy makers think and watching the same economic signals and monetary signposts that they watch. Good Fed watching means anticipating Fed reactions. It emphasizes the sensitive indicators of changes in bank reserve pressures—such as movements in bank borrowings at the Fed discount window, often the first signal of Fed policy shifts.

Fed watching pays off for investors because, more often than not, Fed-induced movements in the Federal funds rate are the dominant influence on rates on money market instruments and bond yields, as well as on stock prices. Thus, when the Fed is expected to ease reserve pressures and push the funds rate lower, the stock and bond markets usually rally. This effect was evident in August 1982 when Fed easing actions triggered investor buying panics in both the bond and stock markets. Again, in late 1985 and early 1986, expectations of imminent Fed easing moves, including possible discount rate cuts, helped mightily in rallying the bond market and pushing stock prices to record highs. Of course, the opposite effect can occur when the Fed moves to tighten reserve pressures and to push interest rates higher.

The following analysis serves as a practical guide for anyone seeking to understand or learn more about Federal Reserve policy and how to forecast interest rates. The emphasis is on the real world of money market trends, actual factors behind Federal Reserve policy shifts, and appropriate adjustments in personal and institutional investment decisions. For the student of monetary policy and interest rate fluctuations, this analysis offers a set of realistic guidelines that Fed officials track closely. These guidelines are indispensable for the Fed watcher because they provide the first clue to future Fed policy shifts and related interest rate movements.

*A*cknowledgements

Special thanks for comments and advice on this project are owed to C. Richard Youngdahl, retired Chairman of Aubrey G. Lanston & Co. Inc. and a former senior staff member of the Federal Reserve Board of Governors; Lyle Gramley, former member of the Federal Reserve Board of Governors and currently chief economist of the Mortgage Bankers Association; Myron Kandel, financial editor and economics analyst for the Cable News Network; and Ben Russell, President of the New York Institute of Finance, who prodded me into starting this project. Also providing invaluable insight and suggestions were Peter Sternlight, Executive Vice President, and Manager for Domestic Operations, System Open Market Account, Federal Reserve Bank of New York; Michael Prell, Deputy Director of Research, Federal Reserve Board of Governors; Howard Lee, Staff Director, U.S. House Subcommittee on Domestic Monetary Policy; and my trusted and helpful colleague at Aubrey G. Lanston & Co. Inc, Irving Auerbach. Last but not least, special recognition should be accorded the strong support provided by my staff at Aubrey G. Lanston & Co., including Patricia Thrapp, Frank Figliolino, Ann Costanza, and Margaret Kormanik.

Introduction—
The Basics

Monetary policy is the Government's most flexible policy tool. Through adjustments in bank reserve pressures, Federal Reserve (Fed) policy makers can influence the rate of growth in money and credit. The Fed tightens reserve pressures in order to restrain the rate of increase in the supply of money and credit relative to demands by consumers, businesses, and government. The result will be an increase in interest rates (the cost of money and credit). The ultimate impact will be to curtail economic activity. Conversely, when the Fed eases reserve pressures in order to increase the rate of growth in money and credit relative to demands, interest rates will decline, thus stimulating economic activity. In short, monetary policy, through adjustments in the cost and availability of money and credit, can have a powerful influence, particularly on consumer spending on autos and other "big ticket" items, home buying, and business investment in new plant and equipment.

Under the Federal Reserve Act of 1913, the Federal Reserve System was created to assure, in essence, that financial conditions would be supportive of sustained, noninflationary economic growth.[1] The Federal Reserve System consists of a Board of Governors made up of seven Governors appointed by the President for 14-year terms with the advice and consent of the Senate, and twelve district Federal Reserve Banks.[2] The President also designates a Chairman of the Board of Governors for a 4-year term, that can be renewed at the President's pleasure. The Fed Chairman has traditionally been the most powerful figure in the System; indeed this individual has been, at times, perhaps the second most powerful person in the nation.

The most important Fed policy-making group is the Federal Open Market Committee (FOMC). This Committee consists of the seven members of the Board of Governors plus five voting Federal Reserve Bank Presidents. The FOMC meets on a regularly scheduled basis approximately eight times per year and may call special telephone meetings when conditions dictate. Based on this Committee's assessment of the economic situation and outlook, monetary growth, and international considerations, among other factors, Fed policy-makers may decide to tighten (or ease) bank reserve pressures, thus exerting upward (or downward) pressures on interest rates. For example, if the dominant view among FOMC members is that economic growth is too strong and potentially inflationary, then the majority of Committee members are likely to decide to tighten reserve pressures and exert upward pressures on interest rates. Conversely, if economic growth is slumping, then FOMC members are likely to respond by easing reserve pressures and exerting downward pressures on interest rates. Alternatively, the majority of FOMC members may be satisfied that economic growth is on a sustainable, non-inflationary path and therefore no changes in reserve pressures and interest rates are called for.

The FOMC controls Fed open market operations. Through these open market operations, the Fed provides the lion's share of the bank reserves necessary to support money and credit growth. Additional bank reserves are supplied through the Fed discount "window." Actually, each regional Reserve Bank has its own discount "window" at which depository institutions in that district may, on a temporary basis, borrow reserves. In definitional terms, total reserves less discount window borrowings equals nonborrowed reserves. Requests to change the discount rate paid by depository institutions for the privilege of borrowing at the Fed discount "window" are originated by one or more of the Boards of Directors of the regional Reserve Banks. But the Board of Governors, based on a majority vote, must ultimately decide whether or not to put the requested discount rate changes into effect. (For a typical set of minutes of discount rate deliberations, see Appendix I.) In these Board votes on requested discount rate changes, the Fed Chairman is rarely overruled. One exception occurred behind the scenes in late February 1986 (see Chapter 7).

Total bank reserves consist of excess reserves plus legally required reserves that depository institutions must hold against their deposits. Depository institutions (usually the smaller ones) may hold excess reserves for precautionary purposes, owing to fears over bank failures or a financial crisis, or as a part of their short-term liquidity, available to meet unforeseen increases in loan activity or deposit outflows.

The concept of free (or net-borrowed) reserves represents one measure of the degree of pressure on bank reserve positions. Free (or net-borrowed) reserves are defined as excess reserves less borrowings at the discount window. When excess reserves exceed borrowings the sign of this measure is *positive* and it is called free reserves. The higher the free reserves figure, the less the pressure on bank reserve positions (or the more accommodative is monetary policy). Conversely, when borrowings exceed excess reserves the sign of this measure is negative and it is called net-borrowed reserves. The larger the net-borrowed reserves figure, the greater is the pressure on bank reserve positions (or the more restrictive is monetary policy).

Bank borrowings at the discount window alone can be an even more straightforward indicator of pressure on bank reserve positions, assuming that bank demands for excess reserves are stable or predictable. Indeed, borrowings at the discount window are the key measure of pressure on bank reserve positions used by the FOMC in its policy directives. When the Fed seeks to tighten reserve pressure it raises its target for the banking system's borrowings; when the Fed moves to ease reserve pressure it lowers its target for borrowings. Banks may borrow at the discount window for one of three basic purposes.

Most commonly, individual banks (usually the larger ones) borrow at the discount window for temporary *adjustment* purposes to meet short-term liquidity needs arising from unanticipated loan demands or deposit outflows. Other types of liquidity needs forcing banks to borrow for adjustment purposes might include the need to avoid overdrafts in their reserve accounts at the Fed, or because of unforeseen outside forces such as wire transfer failures.

A second type of bank borrowing at the discount window is for *seasonal* purposes.   For example, banks in tourist areas facing seasonal reserve drains owing to a surge in currency in circulation, or banks in farming areas facing heavy seasonal loan demands for crop planting purposes, might borrow at the discount window for periods of several weeks at a time.

Still another reason for bank borrowing at the discount window is for *extended credit* purposes. However, this demand for lender-of-last-resort borrowings is for longer intervals as in the 1984 Continental Illinois Bank crisis or the 1985 problems of state insured savings and loan associations in Ohio and Maryland. For this reason borrowings for extended credit purposes should be subtracted from total bank borrowings at the discount window in measuring the degree of pressure on bank reserve positions.

In sum, a Fed-induced tightening in pressure on bank reserve positions will result in a rising total for adjustment and seasonal borrowings and an increase in money market interest rates. As a general rule, Federal Reserve policy makers have often been too timid in adjusting reserve pressures and interest rates to counter cyclical excesses. Because of the Fed's natural caution in adjusting reserve pressures and interest rates, it tends to be pro-cyclical; the monetary authorities tend to reinforce economic expansions by being too accommodative and they tend to aid and abet cyclical contractions by being too restrictive.

The encouraging exception to this pattern occurred in the period from October 1979 to October 1982 when the monetary authorities put the System on "automatic pilot." Under this reserve control plan (see Chapter 6), excessive money and credit demands—which at the time were spurred by run-away inflationary psychology and speculative excesses—resulted more or less *automatically* in sharply increasing reserve pressures and an unexpectedly pronounced surge in interest rates. Needless to say, these uncharacteristically powerful counter-cyclical Fed policy moves soon brought the speculators back to reality and helped eliminate inflationary excesses.

This analysis examines in Section I the forcefulness of personalities in the evalution of the Fed policy-making process and the key economic and financial guides that the monetary authorities watch and react to. In Section II, important clues are provided about how the Federal Reserve implements its policy shifts. In Section III, the key indicators of Fed policy shifts are uncovered so that Fed watchers can be first to anticipate interest rate movements and investors can position themselves correctly in the bond and stock markets.

What Does the Fed Watch and React To—And Why?

There are some simple principles to follow in Fed watching. First, get to know the key Fed policy makers' views on policy objectives and policy implementation. Second, realize that the monetary authorities must watch some economic and financial series more closely than others. The 1979–1982 experience proved that the Fed must limit its focus to be effective. In order to fight inflation, the monetary authorities focused on effectively disciplining money (M-1) growth. This effort was based on the simple proposition that high rates of inflation tend, in time, to be associated with high rates of money growth. On a more practical level, the Fed simply realized that all other methods except monetary discipline had been tried and failed. Fiscal restraint certainly could not be counted on to do the job. The focused policy approach worked; by the early 1980s the Fed had achieved a degree of money discipline and the back of inflation was broken. (The Fed's money discipline efforts were aided in the fight against inflation by a stronger dollar, in part a reflection of Fed restraint; declining OPEC prices; rising food production; and an increased margin of excess world productive capacity.)

1

The Fed watcher should also be aware that, to implement their policy decisions, the policy makers have come to focus on certain sensitive indicators of Fed-induced changes in bank reserve pressures, such as bank borrowings at the Fed discount window. Actually, this obscure borrowings figure is the only reserve measure routinely targeted by Fed policy makers to convey Federal Open Market Committee (FOMC) meeting decisions to the Manager for Domestic Operations, System Open Market Account. This Manager, based at the New York Reserve Bank, is responsible for implementing FOMC directives.

Institutionally, the Federal Reserve System is divided into two major power centers—the Board of Governors in Washington D.C., and the 12 regional Reserve Banks (Boston, New York, Philadelphia, Richmond, Atlanta, Cleveland, Dallas, Kansas City, Chicago, Minneapolis, St. Louis, and San Francisco). The Presidents of the various Reserve Banks are chosen by their respective Boards of Directors with the approval of the Board of Governors. Traditionally, the New York Reserve Bank has been the most influential among the district Banks. This stems in part from the fact that the President of the New York Reserve Bank has a permanent vote as Vice Chairman of the FOMC, while the remaining 11 district Reserve Banks serve in the remaining 4 voting positions in the FOMC on a rotating basis.

Chapter 1

Personalities and Power

The worst mistake that a Fed watcher can make is to assume that central banking is a science. Those who don't know any better assert that somewhere there exists a secret formula. Following such a script, all that monetary authorities have to do is to set the reserve pressure "dial" properly and the result will be just the right amount of money and credit growth necessary to support the right pace of healthy but noninflationary economic growth.

Nothing could be further from the truth. Central banking is an art, not a science; it is practiced by real people, not robots, who want room to maneuver, not rules. Actual policy implementation is a reactive process involving continuous trial and error, a never-ending process of observation and adjustment. Moreover, Fed policy makers are constantly subjected to a barrage of outside influences. To name just a few: Wartime financing constraints were placed on the Fed in World War II when interest rates were pegged, and during the Vietnam War the Johnson Administration deliberately understated the size of the defense spending build-up. Also, the Fed is affected by the profound fiscal irresponsibility of Congress and mounting pressures to monetize the mountain of federal debt required to finance a runaway deficit. In addition, the Fed must cope with major bank failures, farm credit problems, and problems with bank loans to less-developed countries. If this were not enough, there are oil embargoes and food shortages, not to mention foreign trade problems and the related threat of protectionism.

In this environment, Fed leaders are molded as men make steel, in the fire. The best Fed leaders have risen up in challenging times, not unlike Winston Churchill in wartime Britain or Franklin Roosevelt during the depression. The subjective art of central banking requires, in addition to at least some technical knowledge, good instincts and a feel for policy timing, qualities that may be more inbred than acquired.

By these standards, there have been four outstanding Fed leaders: Benjamin Strong, Marriner Eccles, William McChesney Martin, Jr., and Paul Volcker. In each case, the Fed official had the perception and instinct to identify the major economic problem at hand and the vision and persistence to deal with it effectively. For Strong, the problem was how to properly exercise the newly found tools and techniques of Fed policy. For Eccles, it was the instinctive recognition that monetary policy does not take place in a vacuum, and that fiscal stimulation was needed to overcome the depression. For Martin, the problem was how to sustain post–World War II growth and prosperity without an outburst of inflation. And for Volcker, it was how to effectively contain rampant and ingrained inflationary pressures.

Of course, Fed leaders benefit from the fact that monetary policy is more flexible than fiscal policy. The Fed's discretion in adjusting its monetary policy stance can be virtually limitless; Congress' effective discretion in adjusting fiscal policy is, by contrast, next to nonexistent. Because of its relative independence, the Fed can, at least for a time, counter the thrust of fiscal policy and thereby thwart Washington's political excesses. In effect, this makes a strong Fed leader the second most powerful person in the country.

Benjamin Strong

It is no exaggeration to assert that Benjamin Strong, Governor of the Federal Reserve Bank of New York, was as important to the early development of the Federal Reserve System as George Washington was to the development of our country. Strong had no formal college education, but he had extensive commercial banking and trust experience before coming to the New York Reserve Bank. In a lasting legacy, Strong shaped and influenced the Fed in its formative years from 1913 to 1928.

Almost as if by instinct, Strong always saw the big monetary policy picture. This breadth of vision was touchingly illustrated in a note he wrote and kept in the top drawer of his desk:

> "To the Governor of the Federal Reserve Bank of New York:
>
> 'Never forget that it [the Federal Reserve Bank of New York] was created to serve the employer and the working man, the producer and the consumer, the importer and the exporter, the creditor and the debtor, all in the interest of the country as a whole.' "[1]

In keeping with his big-picture approach, Strong, together with the powerful Montagu Norman, Governor of the Bank of England, was the principal architect of world monetary reconstruction after World War I. Strong was also a leader in international central bank cooperation; his efforts in this direction included practical items such as the earmarking of gold, investment of deposits, and the regular exchange of information on current developments in the financial markets. More important was the financial cooperation between central banks required for currency stabilization. For example, in early 1925 Strong informed Norman that a Federal Reserve discount rate increase to 3½% from 3% was imminent. To protect sterling, Norman coordinately raised the British discount rate to 5% from 4%.[2]

In the meantime, Strong was one of the first Fed officials to recognize and understand the significance of the new Fed policy tool discovered in the early 1920s—open market operations. He saw clearly that in order to sterilize gold inflows, the Fed must reduce its holdings of government securities. Incredibly, Fed officials discovered the reserve-supplying potential of open market operations more or less by accident, as the various regional Federal Reserve Banks increased their holdings of government securities in order to use the interest earned to pay for increasing operating expenses.[3] Fortunately, this source of income—which the Fed continues to rely on to this day to meet expenses—is independent of the Federal budget process, and thereby reinforces the Fed's operational independence as an agency of Congress.

Strong argued vigorously against Washington legislation proposing that the Fed be required to impose direct price controls. He asserted that price levels are affected by many factors beyond the Fed's control (e.g., the capacity utilization rate, wage rates, productivity). Strong correctly held that the Fed's job is instead to control credit, something more within its grasp.[4] By disciplining credit growth, the Fed could moderate inflationary pressures.

Marriner S. Eccles

Marriner S. Eccles from Utah was another Fed leader who displayed uncommon vision and purpose in a crisis. Son

of a Scotsman who had come to the U.S. penniless, Marriner Eccles seemed an unlikely candidate for greatness.
Despite no formal college education, he gained wide experience as a leader in major Utah banking and sugar operations. After a brief stint in Washington as a special
assistant to Secretary of the Treasury Henry Morgenthau,
Marriner Eccles was named Chairman of the Federal Reserve Board by President Roosevelt on November 10, 1934.

   The greatest insights of Marriner Eccles came when
they were needed most, during the depression years of
the 1930s. He was among the first to advocate an active
fiscal policy to fight the depression. Eccles was fully aware
that an "excess of federal expenditures over tax collections
tends to increase incomes."[5] He argued that such a
stimulative fiscal policy should be used to "moderate and
offset declines in business."[6] At the same time, Eccles argued appropriately that an excess of tax collections over
federal expenditures—fiscal restraint—should be used to
moderate the rate of business expansion.

   Eccles favored an "active easy-money policy." Specifically, he felt that the Fed should purchase a large volume
of government obligations to permit an "increase in deposits and excess reserves of member banks, which enable
them to take up additional amounts of government securities and in the process create further new deposits."[7] In
essence, Eccles saw to it that the banking system had
plenty of funds. Thus, during most of the depression, the
weakness in consumer and business credit expansion was
not the result of a lack of lendable bank funds. Rather it
was the unwillingness of banks and borrowers alike to
take the *risks* inherent in lending and borrowing in a
highly uncertain environment.

   Regarding general policy objectives, Eccles determined that the problem of controlling booms and depres-
sions is a major part of any country's policy agenda. He
stated succinctly that, "the problem is to provide for the
nation the largest possible real income, in terms of goods
and services, and to have this income distributed between
current consumption and investment as to provide for a

continuous flow of goods from farm and mine and factory to consumers."[8]

On the foreign front, recognizing the need for central bank discretion, Eccles argued in favor of foreign exchange intervention. "We must not permit ourselves to be tied to a rigidly automatic gold standard that makes us helpless against the impact of forces from abroad."[9]

On the domestic banking front, Eccles made major contributions in bringing bank deposit insurance and banking reform to speed recovery and avoid future financial crises. The Banking Act of 1935 was a monument to Eccles' tenacity and advanced understanding of how the nation's banking structure should function. He overcame entrenched banking interests and set up a banking system that operated in the public interest.

Most importantly, in the twilight years of his Fed career (1948–1951), Eccles fought tirelessly for Federal Reserve independence from the Treasury. Eccles, who stayed on as a Fed Governor even though President Truman did not redesignate him as Fed Chairman in 1948, insisted that the financing of Treasury debt at pegged interest rates had made the Fed an "engine of inflation." As aptly stated by Eccles at a special FOMC meeting on February 6, 1951,

> "We should publicly inform the President, the Treasury, and the Congress of what we propose to do, and then do it. Otherwise the public will get the impression that we have capitulated and lack the courage to discharge our responsibilities. If Congress objects to our actions it can change the law; but until it does that, we have a clear responsibility to check inflation—insofar as we can do this within the framework of our authority—by preventing a further growth in the supply of money and credit at this time."[10]

In essence, Eccles was arguing that the Fed should be given complete freedom to carry out its vital policy duties of limiting money and credit growth to fight inflation. Accordingly, it should be left to market forces to determine interest rate levels and thus the shape of the yield curve.

In the end, Eccles should be given most of the credit for the important Accord between the Federal Reserve and the Treasury on March 4, 1951, which freed the Fed from pegging yields on government securities. This Accord was perhaps the most important blow struck for Fed independence in the entire period since World War II.

The details of Eccles' role in this historic event are fascinating.[11] Eccles showed uncommon courage following an unprecedented meeting between the entire FOMC and President Truman on January 31, 1951. At this meeting, requested by the President, only a general discussion took place in which President Truman stated that he needed to maintain confidence in government's "credit" and in government securities in order to make his foreign policy efforts effective. The President especially emphasized his fight against Russian expansionism. The FOMC, represented by Chairman McCabe, agreed to consult frequently with the Secretary of the Treasury but did not promise to continue to peg interest rates on government securities. In an apparently deliberate distortion of the discussions at this meeting, Treasury Secretary Snyder promptly, on February 1, released a statement to the wire services, wrongly suggesting that the FOMC had agreed to continue to peg interest rates on government securities. Eccles, after careful thought, without the knowledge of the other members of the FOMC, released to the press on February 3 an internal Fed memorandum of the meeting, prepared by Fed Governor Evans and Board Secretary Carpenter. This memo confirmed that the FOMC had made no promises regarding the pegging of government securities yields. The public attention given Eccles' forthright statement of the truth about this meeting appeared to be largely responsible for goading the Treasury (represented in the Accord negotiations by, of all people, William McChesney Martin, Jr.) into a follow-up series of discussions with the Fed that led directly to the important Accord.

William McChesney Martin, Jr.

It would be difficult to imagine anyone who could have carried the art of central banking any further than William McChesney Martin, Jr. He was a consummate consensus-taker among Fed policy makers; but the "consensus" was usually skillfully shaped to fit his own view of the appropriate policy course. Martin, who was the youthful head of the New York Stock Exchange before moving to Washington, based his policy decisions on intuition and feel, along with a good knowledge of institutional arrangements and markets.

Rumor has it that Martin, who at the time was serving in the U.S. Treasury Department, was called in by President Truman and offered the Chairmanship of the Federal Reserve Board, but on the condition that Martin continue to peg government bond rates (as had been done to facilitate Treasury borrowing to finance the war). Apparently, President Truman had suffered personal losses in bonds and wanted to prevent a recurrence. As the story goes, Martin first turned down Truman's offer because the condition was unacceptable. Eventually, agreement was reached, and on April 2, 1951, Martin assumed his duties as Chairman of the Federal Reserve Board.

Martin reigned as Fed Chairman for a record 19 years (1951–1970). During that long tenure, Martin gave new meaning to the tenet that Fed policy makers should not be too specific about methods and goals in order to leave maximum freedom to maneuver.

On the subject of the need to be vigilant against inflation, however, Martin did not mince any words.

> "No greater tragedy, short of war, could befall the free world than to have our country surrender to the easy delusion that a little inflation, year after year, is either inevitable or tolerable. For that way lies ultimate economic chaos and incalculable human suffering that would undermine faith in the institutions of free men."[12]

According to Martin, the broad and purposely vague Fed objectives should be to promote monetary and credit conditions that will foster sustained economic growth together with stability in the value of the dollar. If economic growth appears too strong, the Fed should "lean against the wind" *by restraining bank credit growth;* if economic growth should weaken, the Fed should "lean" the other way. Martin warned that economic interpretation is complicated by the fact that even in a period of broad advance and upward pressures on prices, there may be lulls when conditions seem to be stabilizing and the next turn of events is difficult to appraise.

In a gem of wisdom for future Fed Chairmen, Martin emphasized that Fed policy should be concerned with the entire economy and not individual sectors. He said:

> "The work of the System requires a continuous study and exercise of judgement in order to be alert to the way the economy is trending and what Federal Reserve actions will best contribute to sustained growth. Credit policy must, however, fit the general situation and not reflect unduly either the condition of certain industries experiencing poor business or that of other industries enjoying a boom."[13]

In discussing the need to limit money growth to fight inflation in the late 1950s, Martin provided some penetrating insights into the inflation process.

> "A spiral of mounting prices and wages seeks more and more financing. It creates demands for funds in excess of savings and since these demands cannot be satisfied in full, the result is mounting interest rates and so-called tight money. If the gap between investment demands and available savings should be filled by creating additional bank money, the spiral of inflation which tends to become cumulative and self-perpetuating would be given further impetus."[14]

In essence, Martin's approach to controlling inflationary pressures through money and credit restraint was, in his own expression, to take the punch bowl away before the party gets too wild. Under Martin, recurring periods of monetary restraint in the second half of the 1950s set the stage for a "golden age" of economic growth with low inflation in the first half of the 1960s. The Martin "magic" suddenly disappeared in the second half of the 1960s, however, when the Fed became too accommodative. At that time, the Johnson Administration was trying to pay for the Vietnam War, at least initially, without raising taxes. When the tax increase finally came in 1968, the Fed compounded the error by easing prematurely, on the mistaken expectation that the tax increase would promptly depress economic activity.[15]

Paul Volcker

It has been said that Paul Volcker was born to be Fed Chairman.[16] By training and temperament, if not appearance, he is the central banker's central banker. To an unprecedented degree, Volcker's policy mastery has ranged from the technical intricacies of day-to-day Fed open market operations to the highest intellectual levels of monetary policy conception. As a high-level policy technician, Volcker's sense of policy, purpose, and timing—at least over the critical five-year period from late 1979 through late 1984—has been unmatched in the annals of central banking.

In July 1979, when President Jimmy Carter decided to shake up his cabinet, he needed a replacement for the then Fed Chairman G. William Miller, who was being appointed Treasury Secretary to replace W. Michael Blumenthal. As the story goes, when President Carter called Treasury Undersecretary Anthony Solomon to ask whom he should appoint, Solomon recommended Volcker. "Who is he?" the President was reported to have asked.[17]

On July 25, 1979, President Carter announced that

Paul Volcker would be the new Fed Chairman. Volcker's training had been perfect for the job. After graduation from Princeton University and graduate training at Harvard and the London School of Economics, Volcker began his career as an economist at the Federal Reserve Bank of New York. Some experience in the commercial banking sector followed, after which Volcker went to Washington in 1962 as Director of Financial Analysis in the Treasury Department. He was promoted to Treasury Deputy Undersecretary for Monetary Affairs in 1963. After more commercial banking experience, Volcker returned to Washington in a much more important role, to serve from 1969 to 1974 as Treasury Undersecretary for Monetary Affairs. Traveling from one major foreign capital to another, he served as the principal U.S. negotiator in the international monetary talks that followed the collapse of the Bretton Woods system of fixed exchange rates. To round out his training, Volcker was President of the New York Fed from 1975 to 1979.

As Fed Chairman, Volcker faced the seemingly insurmountable challenges of a slumping U.S. dollar and violent and imbedded inflation. Volcker's immediate predecessor—G. William Miller—had made a pitifully weak response to these challenges.

But the answer was about to be found in Volcker, the ultimate policy pragmatist. To be sure, it took some initial trial and error, including an ill-fated and thankfully brief Carter Administration flirtation with credit controls (from March to July 1980).

Nevertheless, Volcker's approach to countering inflation and strengthening the dollar was sound. He started with the proposition that, over long periods of time, excessive inflationary pressures are associated with excessive monetary growth. In his own words: "A basic premise of monetary policy is that inflation cannot persist without excessive monetary growth, and it is our view that appropriately restrained growth of money and credit over the longer run is critical to achieving the ultimate objectives of reasonably stable prices and sustainable economic growth."[18]

In Volcker's approach, money growth targets served more as a practical discipline for monetary policy rather than as the altar at which the monetarist faithful might worship. The "big-bang" move was made at the so-called "Saturday Massacre" on October 6, 1979. At this special Federal Open Market Committee (FOMC) meeting, Fed policy makers, under Volcker's guidance, decided to try to discipline money growth from the supply side by directly controlling reserves rather than from the demand side by controlling the federal funds rate. To be sure, Volcker was undoubtedly aware of Fed staff studies at the time that showed no significant difference in the effectiveness of the two approaches, at least in the month-to-month, or even quarter-to-quarter time context in which monetary policy decisions are made.[19] Nevertheless, Volcker's keen sense of policy significance and timing seemed to suggest the need for a dramatically announced change in operating procedures. Moreover, the funds-rate approach had been tried in the 1970s and found wanting, primarily because of the central bank's natural caution in adjusting the federal funds rate. In essence, the plan had two key advantages: the element of surprise and the potential for much sharper interest rate increases that could eventually damp the speculative appetites of consumer and business borrowers.

The secret to the ultimate success of this ingenious Volcker money control plan was not that it conformed to monetarist doctrine more closely than the Fed had ever done before. Rather, the secret to success was that this plan focused both internal Fed policy-making attention and external Washington political attention on the generally-agreed-upon need for monetary "discipline" to fight inflation. In this way attention was diverted towards monetary growth and away from the Fed's influence on the twin political evils of sharply rising interest rates and a climbing unemployment rate which inevitably accompanied Fed tight money policies. As a result, "market forces" could be blamed for these twin evils. This was a far cry from the period when the Fed was targeting the federal funds rate and a political hue and cry was set off every time interest rates inched upward even by as little as one-eighth of a percentage point.

Of course, in the tradition of central banking as an art not a science, there was plenty of room for discretion under Volcker's plan—and he used all of it. In essence, while Volcker viewed the need for monetary discipline as indispensable, he reserved the right to change money growth targets, or to shift emphasis from M-1 to the broader aggregates when conditions warranted. Discretionary actions were taken in 1983 and again in 1985 when the Fed rebased money growth so as to tolerate more money growth than otherwise would have been the case. The point is that the money-discipline plan, combined with Volcker's intellectual persuasiveness and exquisite feel for policy, *worked*—it helped to contain inflation and strengthen the U.S. dollar.

No doubt Volcker will leave his most important mark on history by the unique forcefulness of his personality. The man is a study in contrasts. Personally, he is unassuming, approachable, informal, and slightly ruffled in appearance, like a traveling salesman who spends too much time in one suit of clothes. Yet, as the chief architect of monetary policy, and perhaps the best-known and most influential financial figure of his time, his very presence is at once magisterial, confident, and awe inspiring; the man exudes competence. Volcker's hidden motives pervade FOMC directives and official Fed statements, and result in language that is often unusually obscure, even by Fed standards. A classic example of this carefully crafted ambiguity was seen in Volcker's February 1985 Humphrey-Hawkins testimony when he presented M-1 growth targets on two distinctly different bases. Without stating that his motives were to avoid a premature Fed tightening response to above-target M-1 growth and concurrently trying not to appear antimonetarist, Volcker established M-1 growth targets for the year 1985 on both the traditional "cone" and on a significantly more liberal "tunnel" (or parallel line) basis (see Chapter 2). Almost certainly, Volcker was seeking more policy flexibility, while giving the appearance of maintaining monetary discipline. As a testament to the force of Volcker's personality, the Congress and the financial public at large accepted the alternative M-1 measurements mostly on faith.

Chapter 2

Fed Visibility Rises

To the average American, Federal Reserve policy shifts are
extremely abstract. The mystical nature of secret policy
meetings, changes in reserve pressures, fluctuations in
bank borrowings at the Fed discount window, and discount rate adjustments would seem to have little, if any-
thing, to do with the average family's ability to put bread
on the table.

Fed Policy Makes Front Page News

In the early 1970s, the Fed planted the seeds that were
destined to grow into a new era of increased public
scrutiny of monetary policy shifts. The first step in this
direction came rather innocently in March 1970 (see Chapter 6) when Fed policy makers began to target a desired
rate of money growth. Inevitably, Fed efforts to keep

money growth on target would mean that interest rates might fluctuate more or less depending on market forces and the Fed's success in stabilizing the economy. In particular, there was, as the 1970s progressed and inflationary pressures mounted, more volatility in the Federal funds rate (the rate on reserves loaned and borrowed among banks, usually overnight). Since the funds rate represents the cost of day-to-day funds for banks and securities dealers, its movements foreshadow changes in the prime lending rate and other money market interest rates. Thus, wider and more frequent movements in the cost of overnight funds triggered wider and more frequent movements in more publicly visible rates such as the prime and the Treasury bill rate. And the Fed discount rate, usually with a lag, also tended to follow these other rates (see Chart 2-1).

During the brief but intense credit crunch of 1973–1974, Fed-induced interest rate movements hit the front pages of newspapers more often than ever before and have remained front page news ever since. The 1973–1974 credit crunch became a newsworthy pocketbook issue for the average American. It was easy to relate to Fed policy shifts because for a brief period they were extreme enough to promptly affect the interest rates that businesses and individual borrowers had to pay. In the wake of Fed moves to tighten bank reserve pressures, the funds rate moved sharply higher and increases in the prime rate, the Treasury bill rate, and other money market rates promptly followed. Even longer-term interest rates got into the tighter-money act. Indeed, the 1973–1974 spike in mortgage rates threw housing activity into a tailspin.

An even more spectacular Fed headline-producing event was the "Saturday Massacre" on October 6, 1979. At this special FOMC policy meeting, the Fed decided to emphasize a direct reserve control approach to implementing monetary policy in order to control monetary growth more effectively at a time of surging speculative borrowing demands and soaring inflation psychology. At the same

CHART 2-1
Selected interest rates (monthly 1970–1985)

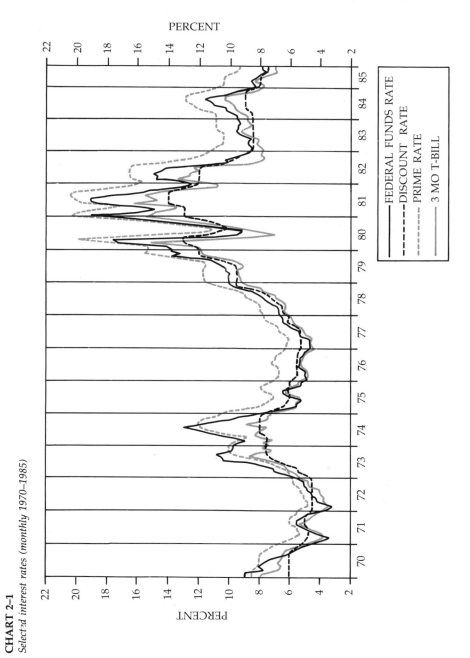

PERCENT

FEDERAL FUNDS RATE
DISCOUNT RATE
PRIME RATE
3 MO T-BILL

PERCENT

time, the Fed decided to tolerate much wider fluctuations
in interest rates. These restrictive Fed actions helped push
the prime rate to a record 21.5% in 1981. The Fed was
again thrust dramatically to the center of public attention.
Prohibitively high borrower rates led to a deep and pro-
longed recession, and to a surge in the unemployment rate
to the highest level since the Great Depression.

Weekly M-1 Watch

For present-day Fed watchers, a most interesting feature
of the trend toward greater publicity surrounding Fed actions is the weekly M-1 watch.[1] At 4:30 P.M. eastern standard time each Thursday, the release time for Fed money
supply figures and other weekly Fed data, ticker tape
watchers abound, hoping for clues to the Fed's next policy
move.

During weeks when M-1 growth surges above the
Fed's annual target range, the overriding market concern
is that the monetary authorities may respond by tightening reserve pressures and pushing interest rates higher.
This Fed tightening prospect usually (except in periods
when accelerating inflation is feared and Fed restraint is
welcomed) tends to depress bond, and often, stock market
sentiment. Conversely, during weeks in which M-1
growth falls below the Fed's annual target range, the market speculates on Fed moves to counter this money
shortfall by easing reserve pressures and pushing interest
rates lower. This Fed easing prospect usually helps rally
the bond market, and often the stock market takes its cue
accordingly.

Legislative Mandate

The glare of publicity surrounding monetary policy actions
was heightened by legislative mandate with a concurrent

Congressional resolution in 1975, and by the passage of the Full Employment and Balanced Growth (Humphrey-Hawkins) Act in 1978. This law requires the Fed to report to Congress semiannually (February and July) on the Fed's analysis of the economy and its targets for monetary and credit growth. This Fed semiannual Humphrey-Hawkins testimony has taken on a circuslike atmosphere with extensive TV coverage, crowded Congressional hearing rooms, and the press and financial markets hanging on every word uttered by the Fed Chairman, who routinely presents the Fed's case at these sessions.

TABLE 2-1
Weekly M–1 levels: targets★ and actual for 1985
(billions of dollars)

Week Ending	3% Lower Limit			8% Upper Limit	
	Cone	Tunnel	Actual	Cone	Tunnel
7/1	585.0	579.6	596.1	588.9	594.2
7/8	585.3	580.2	596.6	589.8	594.8
7/15	585.6	580.8	591.8	590.7	595.4
7/22	586.0	581.5	595.5	591.6	596.1
7/29	586.3	582.1	596.8	592.5	596.5
8/5	586.5	582.7	602.1	593.4	597.3
8/12	587.0	583.3	603.1	594.3	597.9
8/19	587.3	583.9	605.8	595.1	598.5
8/26	587.6	584.5	608.3	596.0	599.1
9/2	588.0	585.1	609.5	597.0	599.7
9/9	588.3	585.8	613.7	597.8	600.4
9/16	588.7	586.4	610.2	598.7	601.0
9/23	589.0	587.0	609.7	599.6	601.6
9/30	589.3	587.7	614.8	600.5	602.2
10/7	589.7	588.3	611.9	601.4	602.8
10/14	590.0	588.8	605.1	602.3	603.4
10/21	590.3	589.4	613.6	603.2	601.1
10/28	590.7	590.1	611.4	604.1	604.7
11/4	591.0	590.7	612.1	605.0	605.3
11/11	591.3	591.3	613.6	605.9	605.9

★ Targets computed on traditional growth "cone" basis and on a somewhat more liberal "tunnel" or parallel line basis.

Source: Federal Reserve, Board of Governors; Aubrey G. Lanston & Co., Inc.

Weekly M-1 Scorecard

Fed watchers can keep a "scorecard" on weekly M-1 movements by translating the Fed's target range for annual M-1 growth into upper and lower ranges for weekly M-1 levels (see Appendix II). Note in Table 2–1, for example, that when translated into weekly levels, the Fed's liberalized 3–8% target range for M-1 growth in the second half of 1985 (measured on both a "cone" and "tunnel" basis) was greatly exceeded, especially in August and September of that year. This undesirably strong M-1 growth triggered modest Fed moves to tighten reserve pressures in August and again in September.

Chapter 3

Economic Objectives

The Federal Reserve's longer-term economic objectives are straightforward. These objectives, expressed in general terms in the Employment Act of 1946 (" . . . to promote maximum employment, production, and purchasing power"),[1] were updated in more specific terms in the Humphrey-Hawkins Act of 1978. Ideally, the Fed seeks to attain the policy goals of full employment, stable prices, sustained economic growth, and equilibrium in the foreign exchange value of the dollar.

The Humphrey-Hawkins Act also provided the "medium-term" goal of within five years reducing the unemployment rate for individuals aged 16 and over to 4% and established the goal of reducing the inflation rate to no more than 3%.[2]

Conflict in Objectives

A policy bias that favors one of these objectives makes it more difficult to attain some of the other objectives, at least over the short run. The Humphrey-Hawkins Act ostensibly recognized this potential conflict and insisted that the "policy and programs for reducing the rate of inflation are to be designed so as not to impede achievement of the goals and timetable for the reduction of unemployment." Clearly, more is required to accomplish this difficult task than the mere stroke of a legislative pen.

In any case, throughout most of the post–World War II period (i.e., 1945–1979), the primary national economic policy emphasis was on full employment. Starting in the late 1960s, however, policy efforts to reduce the civilian unemployment rate were made all the more difficult by the fact that demographic factors were ratcheting the unemployment rate upward in each successive business cycle. Specifically, there was a flood of young workers (postwar babies) and women into the labor force. The unemployment rate among these initially inexperienced workers tends to be higher than for the labor force as a whole.

The problem during most of the 1945–1979 period was that recurring doses of expansionary fiscal and monetary policies aimed at full employment made it more difficult to contain inflation. The unemployment rate was pushed to a low of about 3½% in 1966 and again in 1968 (see Chart 3–1). As a result, inflationary pressures accelerated in the late 1960s (see Chart 3–2). This jump in inflation was aggravated by the Vietnam War buildup.

The policy emphasis on full employment was perhaps most damaging in the 1970s. The unemployment rate was pushed down toward 4% in 1973 and inflationary pressures erupted. Again in 1978–1979, the unemployment rate was pushed sharply lower and inflation accelerated. The inflationary spurt in the 1970s was also exacerbated by external forces—including the oil embargo and food shortages.

So far in the 1980s, the policy focus has been on sufficient monetary restraint to contain inflationary pressures once and for all. In some foreign industrial economies

PERCENT

CHART 3–1
Civilian unemployment rate (1955–1985 monthly)

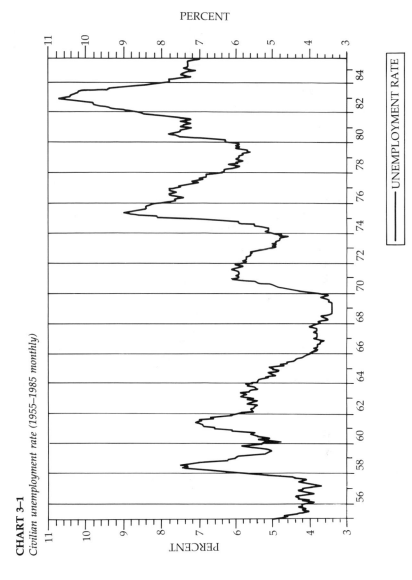

——— UNEMPLOYMENT RATE

PERCENT

CHART 3–2
Consumer inflation (1955–1985 measured on a year-over-year percent change basis)

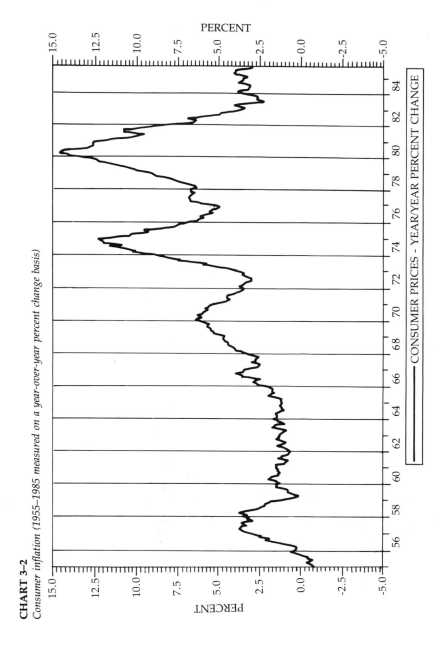

CONSUMER PRICES - YEAR/YEAR PERCENT CHANGE

such as Britain and West Germany, this monetary restraint has been reinforced by fiscal restraint. Although trying to snuff out the last breath of inflation may be a commendable objective, it has tended to damp the 1983–1985 world recovery and to leave unemployment, particularly in major European economies, at undesirably high levels.

Reagan Economics

Amazingly, in 1983 and 1984, the Reagan Administration was able to attain the twin policy objectives of a pronounced decline in inflation and a declining unemployment rate. This success stemmed largely from an accidental policy mismatch between strong fiscal stimulus and monetary restraint (see Chapter 10).

Unfortunately, these commendable goals were achieved at the cost of a dramatic deterioration in the U.S. balance of payments position. The chain of causation unfolded as follows: The clash between monetary restraint and fiscal stimulus (including large tax cuts and spending increases, particularly in defense) produced abnormally high real interest rates; this upward pressure on real rates was heightened by inadequate domestic savings. The relatively high U.S. real rates led to a dramatic strengthening in the U.S. dollar as foreign savers sought U.S. investments carrying these attractive returns and the strong dollar, in turn, led to a huge trade deficit as U.S. exports became more expensive and imports became less expensive (see Chart 3–3). The disturbing implication of this causal chain was that foreign competition threatened eventually to depress U.S. manufacturing and agricultural activity to a point that would stop the U.S. expansion in its tracks. On the political front, this threat triggered an emotional outburst of protectionism, unparalleled in intensity since the days of the 1929 Smoot-Hawley tariff and the Great Depression.

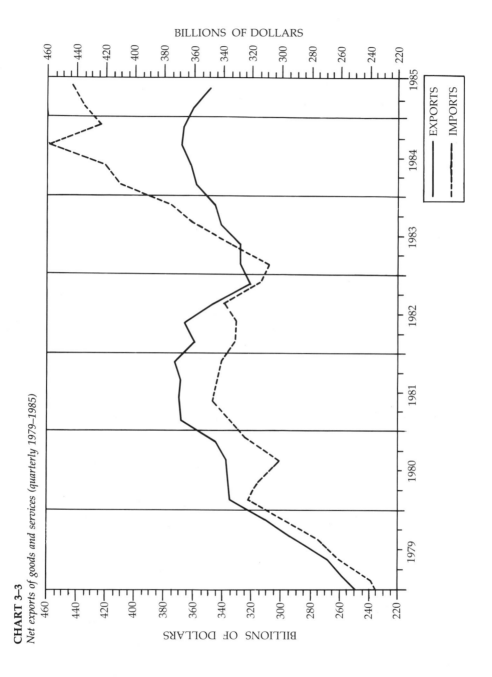

CHART 3-3
Net exports of goods and services (quarterly 1979–1985)

BILLIONS OF DOLLARS

EXPORTS
IMPORTS

Real GNP Focus

For Fed watchers this discussion of economic objectives can be distilled down to just one important item, representing the entire economy rather than individual sectors, and to be included in a practical Fed watching tool kit. This item is quarterly real GNP growth, preferably for the latest quarter and on a projected basis, for the quarter ahead. This measure of aggregate domestic output provides the best indication of the degree of pressure on U.S. domestic productive capacity and, therefore, of potential inflationary strains.

In using this "tool kit" item, Fed watchers should follow a 2, 4, 6 rule. That is, if quarterly real GNP *growth* (at an annual rate) should fall to 2% or below, the Fed could be expected to respond by easing bank reserve pressures and pushing interest rates lower. By this means, the monetary authorities would seek to counter the threat of rising unemployment and a possible economic downturn. Conversely, if quarterly real GNP growth should surge to 6% or above, the Fed may respond by tightening reserve pressures and pushing interest rates higher. This would represent a Fed effort to counter excessive strains on domestic productive resources and the threat of increasing inflationary pressures. Ideally, the monetary authorities would prefer a more sustainable, longer-term growth rate of approximately 4% in real GNP; or possibly a lower estimate for potential growth depending on trends in productivity and labor force growth. In that case, with other things being equal, the Fed could maintain a stable policy stance.

Strains on Productive Capacity

The industrial capacity utilization rate can be used to confirm that a rapid 6% or higher growth rate in real GNP has lasted long enough to begin to exert major strains on productive resources and to pose a major threat of accelerating inflation. This is perhaps the best measure of increasing strains on domestic productive resources—in addition, of course, to a low and declining civilian labor force unemployment rate.

The most commonly used measure of industrial capacity utilization is provided by the Federal Reserve Board.[3] In essence, this measure reflects the *actual* rate of increase in industrial production, relative to net additions to capacity. The productive capacity measure reflects increases in real business capital spending, *less* estimates of the amount of capital stock being depreciated as it becomes obsolete.

As a general rule, the rate of industrial capacity utilization tends to increase sharply early in periods of economic recovery, when actual industrial output is growing rapidly (see Chart 3–4). In the more advanced stages of each cyclical expansion, the capacity utilization rate then peaks out, usually after reaching a level of 87–90%— where the inflationary threat posed by production shortages and bottlenecks is the greatest. In the late 1960s, the industrial capacity utilization rate reached dangerously high levels of nearly 90%, leading to an acceleration in inflationary pressures. Similarly the rate of capacity utilization soared again in 1971–1973 and again in 1975–1978.

By contrast, the capacity utilization rate tends to fall in recession periods when the pace of industrial production is sluggish or even declining. For example, in the deep 1982 recession, the capacity utilization rate dipped below 70%.

In 1985, there occurred a notably encouraging exception to this pattern in which the capacity utilization rate climbs to potentially inflationary levels in the more mature phases of an economic expansion. The rate of capacity utilization actually drifted lower in 1985, settling comfortably in the vicinity of 80%. Pressures on U.S. domestic

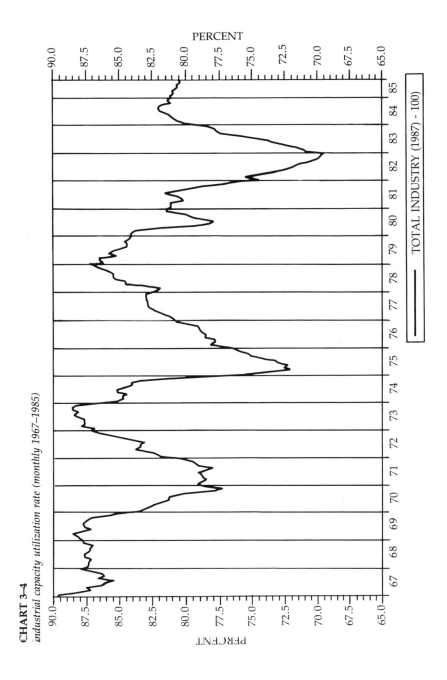

CHART 3-4
industrial capacity utilization rate (monthly 1967–1985)

TOTAL INDUSTRY (1987 - 100)

31

productive capacity were lessened by the fact that, owing to an unusually strong U.S. dollar, brisk U.S. domestic final sales demands (consumer, business and government) were, to an unprecedented extent, spilling over into relatively inexpensive imports. In many instances these imported goods were produced by new and highly efficient foreign productive capacity in basic industries in developing countries in Latin America and Asia. In addition, pressures on U.S. industrial productive capacity were eased by strong domestic business capital spending in 1983 and 1984. To some extent, however, this U.S. business investment was not in capacity-expanding projects and structures but rather in productivity-enhancing equipment aimed at controlling costs or meeting the growing threat of foreign competition.

Chapter 4

Intermediate Federal Reserve Targets

Longer-term objectives such as sustained growth with stable prices represent commendable Federal Reserve concerns. But problems exist because monetary policy is not the only influence on economic activity. Other influences, such as fiscal policy and the foreign trade deficit (as noted in the preceding chapter) can also strongly influence the course of the economy.

Ideally, therefore, the monetary authorities should establish intermediate policy targets that they can control more directly.[1] Of course, these intermediate policy targets should be related to economic activity in a meaningful and predictable manner. Among the candidates for Fed intermediate policy targets are M-1, M-2, and M-3 and the broader credit aggregate (domestic nonfinancial debt).

Traditional Focus on M-1

Although aware that it is less than perfect as an intermediate policy target, Fed officials have tended to focus their attention on the most narrowly defined monetary aggregate—M-1. This money measure consists of the nonbank public's holdings of the most readily spendable funds (currency, demand deposits, and other checkable deposits, including interest-bearing NOW accounts).

Traditionally, the Fed has favored the M-1 aggregate for use in its policy formulation because this aggregate has been the best measure of transactions balances in the hands of the nonbank public. These transactions balances are immediately available to support expenditures on goods and services.

However, over the first half of the 1980s, a major institutional change occurred and this development has at times tended to distort the relationship between money growth and economic activity. As can be seen in Table 4–1, the interest-bearing components of the M-1 aggregate have jumped from 5.1% of M-1 balances in 1980 to a sizable 27.1% in 1985, largely as a result of the introduction of

TABLE 4–1

Interest-bearing components of the monetary aggregates

Aggregate	Interest-Bearing components as a percent of total (percent)	
	1980	*1985*
M-1	5.1	27.1
M-2	76.0	82.6
M-3	80.1	86.1

Note: M-1 interest-bearing components include NOW accounts and other checkable deposits; M-2 interest-bearing components include the interest-bearing components of M-1, plus money market accounts (general purpose and broker-dealer), money market demand deposits, small time and savings deposits, overnight RPs and overnight Eurodollars; M-3 interest-bearing components include all those interest-bearing components in M-2 plus money market accounts (institutional), large time and savings deposits, term RPs and term Eurodollars.

Source: Federal Reserve, Board of Governors; Aubrey G. Lanston & Co., Inc.

highly popular NOW accounts. More importantly, growth in the NOW account component of M-1 has often been extremely volatile, thus distorting M-1 growth and tending to complicate the Fed's efforts to assess the relationship between monetary and economic growth.

This suggests that the public now holds M-1 balances not only for transaction purposes—which are significant from a Fed policy standpoint because they are closely related to the pace of economic activity—but also for savings purposes. Fed policy makers generally attribute less significance to fluctuations in M-1 caused by shifts within savings flows, though these shifts are often difficult to discern. Indeed, these shifts among the forms in which savings are held seem to have little economic significance—other than possibly representing an increase in the proportion of savings held in the most liquid form. The typical move by the public might be to shift funds out of equities or money market investments into the NOW account component of M-1 when rate spreads narrow in favor of these interest-bearing checking accounts.

Broader Aggregates

The monetary authorities, in hopes of reducing distortions, such as those caused by wide fluctuations in NOW account growth, have at times shifted attention to the more broadly defined monetary aggregates such as M-2 and M-3.[2] These broader aggregates are not as distorted as M-1 by extreme volatility in NOW account growth.

The usefulness of these broader aggregates is, however, reduced by the fact that, in a different but significant way, they are highly sensitive to money market rate fluctuations and thus to shifts in savings flows among assets held by individuals. This is because more than 80% of these broader aggregate totals are accounted for by interest-bearing components. This can lead to "perverse" behavior in M-2 and M-3. That is, when the Fed is tightening and pushing interest rates higher, M-2 and M-3 may actually grow more *rapidly*. This could reflect the public's efforts to shift funds out of, say, equities into the higher-yielding money market components of M-2 or M-3. Conversely, a Fed move to ease reserve pressures and push interest rates lower could result in *slower* M-2 and M-3 growth as the public shifts funds in favor of equities and away from the components of these broader aggregates that carry correspondingly lower interest rates.

The still broader credit aggregate (including the debt of the consumer, business, state and local government, and federal government sectors) is more difficult for the Fed to control than the monetary aggregates, since it consists of both bank and nonbank credit.[3] Because of the difficulty in controlling the credit aggregate it would, at present, be inappropriate for the Fed to use this aggregate for policy discipline purposes. Moreover, there have been, particularly during 1984 and 1985, some distortions in the relationship between the two-digit pace of this broader credit aggregate (see Appendix VII) and the single-digit pace of economic activity, reflecting in part the substitution of debt for equity in the business sector. But the fact remains that this broadest of aggregate measures could play an increasingly important role in future Fed policy deliberations as the accuracy and timeliness of data on debt in key sectors improves.

Money Velocity

The relationship between the M-1 aggregate and economic activity is best analyzed in terms of money velocity.[4] Money velocity (or the income velocity of money) is defined as the ratio of nominal GNP to M-1 or, in other words, the number of times money balances have to turn over in any given quarter, in order to support a given level of economic activity. As long as money velocity behaves in a predictable manner, the monetary authorities can target annual M-1 growth and expect that economic activity will behave accordingly in a desired manner.

For example, if the annual average *rate of increase* in money *velocity* is 2.5%, and the Fed sets a 4.5% annual money growth target, then a 7% increase in nominal GNP growth can be generated *without* significant upward pressures on interest rates. As a matter of definition, therefore, the rate of growth of nominal gross national product (GNP) is equal to the rate of increase in money (M) *plus* the rate of increase in velocity (V).[5] Symbolically, this statement can be expressed as:

% change GNP = % change M + % change V

However, if the growth in nominal GNP is 7% but the Fed sets the money growth target at only 3.5%, then velocity must also grow at a 3.5% pace. Short of major institutional or structural changes, however, the only way to increase money velocity is to induce the public to hold smaller money balances in relation to economic activity (GNP) through an increase in *interest rates* on alternative money market investments. Thus, above-trend money velocity growth is most often associated with sharply rising interest rates.

In fact, the *average* quarter-to-quarter gain in money velocity was at an annual rate of about 3% over the period from the mid 1960s to 1980 (see middle horizontal line in Chart 4–1). In addition, at least until the 1980s, the usual *range* of fluctuation in quarter-to-quarter velocity growth was from plus 7½% to minus 1½% (see upper and lower horizontal lines in Chart 4–1).

In the period from 1980 to 1985, however, money velocity growth has registered unusually wide fluctuations, and generally moved downward, in contrast to the rising trend from 1966 to 1980. An unusually sharp swing in money velocity growth occurred in 1980, apparently arising from the brief and unfortunate experience with

CHART 4-1
Velocity of M-1 (quarter-to-quarter percentage change at an annual rate 1966–1985)

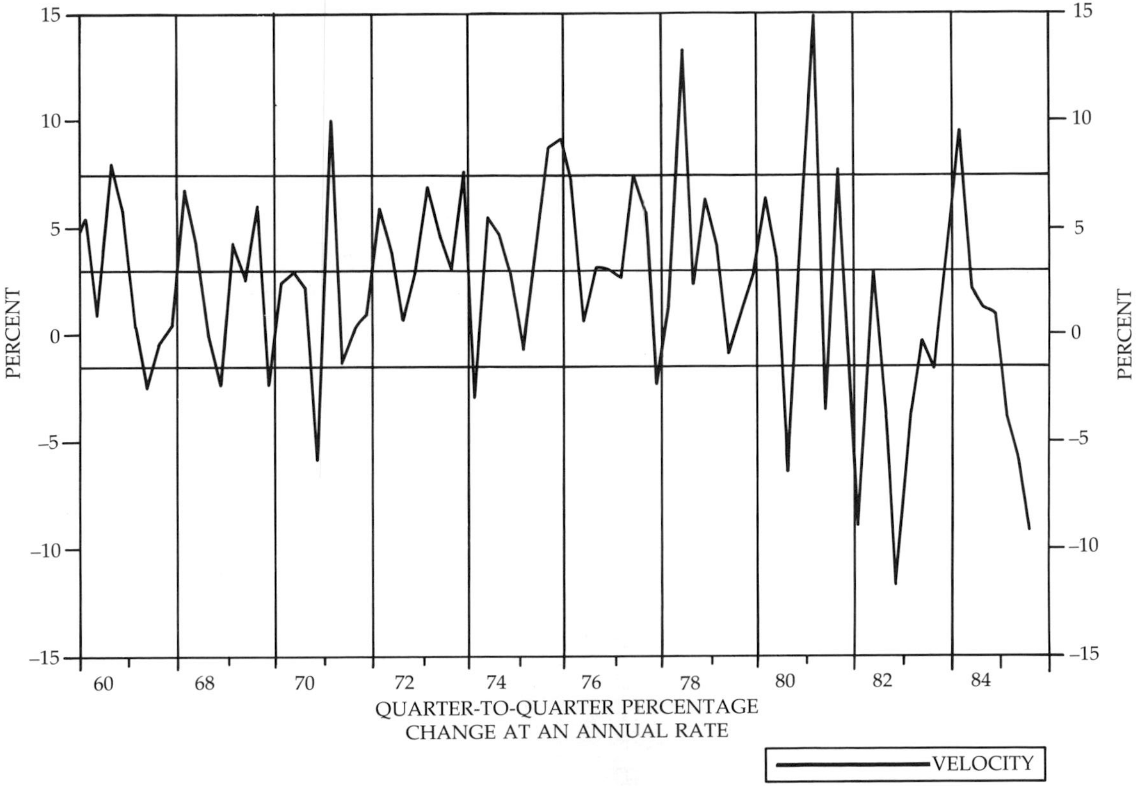

QUARTER-TO-QUARTER PERCENTAGE
CHANGE AT AN ANNUAL RATE

—— VELOCITY

credit controls (imposed only briefly from March through July 1980). Initially these credit controls caused a sharp drop in money velocity at an annual rate of about 6%, as people suddenly became uncertain and increased their money balances, at least relative to the suddenly weakening pace of economic activity. However, credit controls apparently were removed before inflationary psychology and speculative demands were completely snuffed out, and as soon as the credit controls were removed, economic activity surged for a given level of money balances. As a result, money velocity growth exploded at an annual rate of 15%.

A sudden move in the opposite direction occurred in late 1982, when growth in money velocity declined more sharply than normal—in this case at an annual rate of more than 10%. Apparently, in this recessionary period an increasingly uncertain public—facing declining interest rates and an uncertain job market outlook—decided to hold abnormally high money balances in relation to economic activity. Money velocity then promptly surged at nearly a 10% annual rate in early 1984. Most likely, an increasingly confident public—facing rising interest rates on alternative money market investments and an improving employment outlook—decided to hold abnormally low money balances in relation to economic activity.[6]

The unpredictability of money velocity was highlighted again during 1985. Velocity growth showed unexpected declines in each successive quarter.[7] During this period, the rate of growth in GNP was depressed by a deepening foreign trade deficit; at the same time, M-1 growth was soaring.

The unusually wide divergence in 1985 between U.S. final demands (sales) and aggregate domestic output (GNP) resulting from the surge in imports has led some analysts to argue that the economic activity component of the money velocity measure (GNP/M-1) should be modified. Rather than using GNP (aggregate domestic output) as the measure of economic activity in calculating velocity, they have proposed using *final sales to domestic purchasers* (defined as GNP *less* business inventories *less* exports *plus* imports). (See Table 4–2.) This new concept is perhaps less applicable over the longer-term, particularly once the trade deficit shrinks and no longer serves as a depressant on domestic economic output. Nevertheless, the new measure at least takes into account the unusual extent to which money-supported final demands (sales) might, for a time, be spilling over into imports rather than into domestically produced goods.[8]

TABLE 4–2
Selected GNP and final demand concepts
(percentage change at annual rate—1972 dollars)

	1985			
	I	*II*	*III*	*IV*
Gross national product	.3	1.9	3.3[P]	N.A.
Less: Business inventories				
Equals: Final sales	−.3	4.6	5.9	N.A.
Less: Exports				
Plus: Imports				
Equals: Final sales to domestic purchasers	3.4	5.9	5.8	N.A.

P—preliminary.

N.A.—Not available.

Source: E.F. Hutton, *Weekly Economics Letter*, October 21, 1985.

In addition, money demands may have been inflated, particularly in 1985, by a spurt in financial transactions, reflecting mergers, stock proxy fights, and corporate take-overs. This possibility is suggested by the fact that the ratio of debits to demand deposits at New York City banks (at the center of such transactions) grew at a more rapid pace in the second, third, and fourth quarters of 1985 than at other banks, as this special corporate financing activity picked up strongly.[9]

In earlier periods, such as late 1982, because of unpredictable swings in M-1 velocity, Fed policy makers chose to deemphasize M-1 growth in policy deliberations and to place primary policy emphasis on the broader aggregates and on quarterly changes in economic activity. Likewise, during most of 1985, with M-1 velocity declining unexpectedly, the Fed chose to play down the significance of excessive M-1 growth, believing that the surge in this aggregate was transitory.

Despite the difficulties in predicting M-1 velocity, Fed policy deliberations generally place considerable emphasis on money growth, among other factors. The central role of money in Fed policy deliberations is encouraged in part by legislative mandate.

The Humphrey-Hawkins Act of 1978 expressly provides that the Fed transmit to Congress, no later than February 20 and July 20 of each year, a review and analysis of recent developments affecting economic trends. In addition, the Fed is asked to provide the plans and objectives of the Board of Governors and the FOMC regarding the ranges of growth of the monetary and credit aggregates for the calendar year. Further, the legislative mandate requests that the Fed discuss the relation of these monetary and credit growth objectives to short-term goals set forth in the President's Economic Report or approved by Congress.

In practice, however, the monetary authorities have not generally made an effort in their Humphrey-Hawkins testimony to directly link their targets for money and credit growth to the short-term GNP growth objectives of the Administration or of Congress. Instead Fed policy makers (including both voting and nonvoting FOMC members, at least for forecasting purposes) have typically seen fit—perhaps with a view to maintaining their traditional independence—to focus attention on their *own projections* of real GNP, the GNP deflator, nominal GNP, and the unemployment rate. Usually provided are the upper and lower ranges of the Fed policy makers' forecasts and their central tendency (see Table 4–3). At most, the Fed's Humphrey-Hawkins testimony does no more than compare such internal Fed economic forecasts to the latest set of Administration economic forecasts, usually prepared in connection with budget reports or reviews.

TABLE 4-3
Federal Reserve Economic projections for 1985 and 1986★

	FOMC Members and other FRB Presidents		
	Range	Central Tendency	Actual
------1985------			
Percent change, fourth quarter to fourth quarter:			
Nominal GNP	6¼ to 7¾	6½ to 7	5.8
Real GNP	2¼ to 3¼	2¾ to 3	2.8
Implicit deflator for GNP	3½ to 4¼	3¾ to 4	2.9
Average level in the fourth quarter, percent:			
Unemployment rate	6¾ to 7¼	7 to 7¼	7.0
------1986------			
Percent change, fourth quarter to fourth quarter:			
Nominal GNP	5½ to 8½	7 to 7½	N.A.
Real GNP	2 to 4	2½ to 3¼	N.A.
Implicit deflator for GNP	3 to 5½	3¾ to 4¾	N.A.
Average level in the fourth quarter, percent:			
Unemployment rate	6¾ to 7½	6¾ to 7¼	N.A.

★The Administration has yet to publish its mid-session budget review document, and consequently the customary comparison of FOMC forecasts and Adminstration economic goals has not been included in this report.

N.A.—Not Available.

Source: Federal Reserve Board of Governors, *Monetary Policy Report to Congress Persuant to the Full Employment and Balanced Growth Act of 1978,* July 16,1985.

The Fed views its fundamental objective under the Humphrey-Hawkins Act as seeking to prevent excessive monetary stimulus. Yet there remains the technical problem of translating that objective into specific money growth targets, owing to volatility in money velocity. Thus the Fed must exercise judgment in changing these targets. Such special Fed adjustments in its M-1 target base and range occurred in both 1983 and 1985.

For Fed watchers, the relevance of this discussion of the relationship between money and GNP is that it pinpoints a second major item—in addition to quarterly real GNP growth—that should be included in a Fed watching "tool kit." This item is the monthly percentage change (at an annual rate) in the M-1 aggregate for the past month or two, and, on a projected basis, for the month ahead. These actual and projected monthly growth rates in M-1 should, in turn, be compared to the Fed's official annual (and intermediate) target range for M-1 growth in order to help anticipate the next Fed policy shift. [For an example of how the Fed incorporates into its policy directive its intermediate target ranges for growth in the monetary aggregates (usually covering three-month periods) see Appendix IV.]

Hitting (or Missing) the M-1 Target

Because of the short-term volatility in the public's demand for money, and distortions from major institutional changes and innovations in money management, the monetary authorities have not had an easy time hitting their annual target ranges—or even accurately measuring M-1 to see if they did. Indeed, over the decade from 1976 to 1985, the Fed has hit its *annual* target range only three times. As can be seen in Table 4–4 below, the Fed had to adjust for major institutional changes affecting the public's money demands in 1979, 1980, and 1981. In 1979 and 1980, the Fed adjusted the target ranges; in 1981, a critical year in the Fed's anti-inflation efforts, the adjustment was made to the actual M-1 growth figure.

The point is that, contrary to monetarist dogma, few absolutes exist in the art of central banking. About all the monetary authorities could do was to try to exert monetary discipline regarding the *direction* of the rate of money growth, and even this has not always been the case, at least over short periods. Thus, at least in terms of direction, it seemed that M-1 growth became excessive in 1977 and 1978, at annual rates of 7.9% and 7.4%, respectively.

TABLE 4–4

Federal Reserve annual monetary targets and actual growth(percentage change—fourth quarter to fourth quarter,unless otherwise indicated)

Year	Fed M-1 Target	Actual M-1 Growth
1976	4½–7½	5.5
1977	4½–6½	7.9
1978	4 –6½	7.4
1979	3 –6★	5.5
1980	4½–7★	7.3
1981	3½–6	2.1★
1982	2½–5½	8.3
1983	5 –9★★	5.5
1984	4 –8	5.0
1985	3 –8★★	12.1

★Adjusted for effects of shifts of funds into ATS and NOW accounts.

★★Target for second half of year measured from second quarter to fourth quarter.

Note: Actual M-1 growth rates based on unrevised data.

Source: Annual Reports of Manager for Domestic Operations, System Open Market Account (usually in the Spring issues of the Federal Reserve Bank of New York Quarterly Review).

The Fed tried to tighten reserve pressures sufficiently— particularly in the latter part of 1979—to counter this excessive monetary growth. Undoubtedly Fed policy makers welcomed the temporary slowing in money growth in 1979 to 5.5%. In 1980, however, the Fed leaned the wrong way too soon, easing reserve pressures on the heels of a credit-controls-induced drop in money growth and economic activity. This policy mistake was associated with a rebound in money growth to 7.3% in 1980. The Fed then got tough in 1981, tightening reserve pressures aggressively. The problem was that, owing to the nationwide introduction of NOW accounts at the beginning of that year, the monetary authorities were never sure of much more than the *direction* of money growth. They knew that they were tending to reduce the rate of money growth, but exactly how much true money growth was being reduced was difficult to ascertain because the old relationships between money demands, interest rates, and GNP were falling apart.

In this connection, Stephen Axilrod, Staff Director for Monetary and Financial Policy for the Federal Reserve Board of Governors (a key staff position), observed:

"On the demand function for money, I have been in the situation over the years, because my principals are interested in these things, of assessing money–interest rate relationships and of attempting to use money demand functions to that end. I may be exaggerating a little, but every three months or so one finds that a function has been reestimated and that the lags have changed and the interest elasticity has changed. The changes are often sizable, depending on the sample time period. Moreover, there are almost as many differently specified functions as there are flavors of ice cream. And they don't predict too well out of sample periods. This makes one very uneasy about whether the function is inherently stable or predictable. I tend to think something is there that can be grasped, but it is very elusive and leaves scope for, not to say the need for, good judgement on the part of the policy maker."[10]

In late 1982, in the face of deepening recessionary tendencies, not to mention uncertainty about M-1 behavior owing to maturing All-Savers Certificates the monetary authorities moved to de-emphasize M-1 growth in their policy deliberations and to put more emphasis on the broader aggregates. Actual money growth ended that year far above target. The Fed hit its target for the second half of 1983, but only after the monetary authorities had rebased to the second quarter of 1983, thereby tolerating a huge early-1983 M-1 bulge. In July 1985 the Fed again rebased to the second quarter, but even then, actual M-1 growth in the second half of 1985 far exceeded this more liberal target.

Perhaps the Fed's best year targetwise was 1984. In that "golden" year, the monetary authorities hit their M-1 target and did much to strengthen their anti-inflation credibility.

The Art of Money Forecasting

Nothing is more hazardous to an economist's health than forecasting M-1 growth. Truly, M-1 forecasters were created to make meteorologists look good.

Seriously, there are some useful aids in the weekly money supply forecasting game. Money supply forecasters, for example, can use the weekly Chase Bank Deposit Survey. This survey polls a number of money market banks across the country regarding weekly behavior in their demand deposits and other checkable deposits, including NOW accounts. The Chase Deposit survey has a reasonably good track record in forecasting weekly M-1 fluctuations. Unfortunately, the results of this bank deposit survey are routinely available only to participating banks, but they are usually available a day or two before the Thursday release of the weekly M-1 figure from wire services or such press sources as the *Wall Street Journal* or the *New York Times*. Another popular weekly M-1 forecast is provided by *Money Market Services*. This service provides the median weekly M-1 change forecasted by approximately 45 analysts. It, too, has a fairly good track record in forecasting the direction, if not the size, of weekly money supply changes.

Fed watchers should do their own homework as well. Note in the worksheet reproduced in Table 4–5, for example, that a do-it-yourself M-1 forecasting technique might involve estimates of the three major components of M-1 on a not-seasonally-adjusted basis. These forecasts could be founded upon actual weekly movements in currency, demand deposits, and other checkable deposits in the comparable weeks of, say, the previous five years. Once the forecasts of each M-1 component are made on a not-seasonally-adjusted basis, then the seasonal factors, available from the Fed, can be applied to arrive at the final seasonally adjusted weekly M-1 estimate.

TABLE 4–5
Money Forecasting components and seasonal factor
(billions of dollars)

1985		Currency N.S.A.	Seasonal Correction	Estimate	Actual	Other Check Dept. N.S.A.	Demand Deposit N.S.A.	Seasonal Correction	Estimate	Actual	Estimate	Actual
July	1	—	– .2	– .2	+ .2	+1.0	+3.2	– 4.0	+ .2	+3.7	—	+4.0
	8	+3.0	–3.4	– .4	+ .2	+5.0	+5.0	–12.9	–2.9	+ .1	–3.3	+ .2
	15	– .8	+1.1	+ .3	– .4	– .7	—	+ .7	—	–4.5	+ .3	–4.8
	22	– .6	+1.1	+ .5	+ .6	–2.5	–7.5	+10.9	+ .9	+3.1	+1.4	+3.7
	29	–1.0	+1.4	+ .4	+ .5	–1.5	–4.5	+ 8.1	+2.1	+ .8	+2.5	+1.3
August	5	+2.0	–1.3	+ .7	+ .7	+5.0	+7.5	–11.1	+1.4	+4.5	+2.1	+5.3
	12	+ .8	– .7	+ .1	+ .1	+ .5	—	+ 1.5	+2.0	+ .9	+2.1	+1.1
	19	– .7	+1.1	+ .4	+ .5	+ .4	–2.0	+ 3.2	+1.6	+2.4	+2.0	+2.8
	26	–1.0	+1.6	+ .6	+ .4	–2.2	–6.0	+10.1	+1.9	+2.0	+2.5	+2.4
September	2	+ .6	– .6	—	– .1	+1.7	+2.9	– 5.1	– .5	+1.4	– .5	+1.3
	9	+1.2	–1.6	– .4	+ .1	+6.0	+9.0	–12.8	+2.2	+3.6	+1.8	+3.7
	16	–1.0	+1.3	+ .3	+ .3	–3.0	—	+ .6	–2.4	–3.6	–2.1	–3.3
	23	+ .8	+1.1	+ .3	+ .2	–2.5	–9.0	+13.0	+1.5	– .7	+1.8	– .4
	30	– .4	+ .8	+ .4	—	–2.5	—	+ .2	–2.3	+5.3	–1.9	+5.3
October	7	+2.5	–2.8	– .3	+ .3	+5.0	+7.0	–16.2	–4.2	–3.2	–4.5	–2.9
	14	—	—	—	+ .3	–1.0	+2.0	– 1.5	– .5	–6.9	– .5	–6.6
	21	– .5	+1.3	+ .8	+ .4	+1.0	–5.0	+ 7.7	+1.7	+7.9	+2.5	+8.3
	28	–1.0	+1.4	+ .4	+ .3	–1.5	–4.5	+ 9.3	+3.3	–2.4	+3.7	–2.2
November	4	+1.5	–1.3	+ .2	+ .4	+4.0	+10.0	–14.7	– .7	+ .1	– .5	+ .5
	11	+2.0	–1.9	+ .1	+ .2	+2.0	+1.5	+ .2	+3.7	+1.3	+3.8	+1.5
	18	– .5	+ .7	+ .2	– .3	–1.0	+2.0	+ .3	+1.3	+3.1	+1.5	+2.8
	25	– .6	+ .6	—	+ .2	–1.5	–5.6	+11.1	+4.0	+4.2	+1.6	+4.4
December	2	+1.0	– .9	+ .1	+ .8	+1.0	+8.5	– 6.9	+2.6	+4.4	+2.7	+5.3
	9	+1.5	–1.4	+ .1	+ .1	+4.5	+2.0	– 9.6	–3.1	–3.3	–3.0	–3.2
	16	—	+ .4	+ .4	+ .1	–1.0	+2.0	+ .6	+ .4	– .4	+ .8	– .6
	23	+1.0	–1.1	– .1	+ .2	–2.0	+1.0	+ 3.0	+2.0	+5.2	+1.9	+5.3
	30	–1.0	+1.0	—	—	—	+2.5	– 5.8	–3.3	–3.2	–3.3	–3.1

Source: Federal Reserve, Board of Governors; Aubrey G. Lanston & Co., Inc.

M-1 Component Analysis

In addition, Fed watchers might analyze recent unusual movements in M-1 by component. Such an approach might help determine whether a recent spurt in M-1 growth is transitory, and thus not worthy of a Fed tightening response, or permanent, and therefore worthy of closer attention.

The usefulness of analyzing M-1 by component is evident in Table 4–6 below. It could be argued, for example, that the 13.4% (annual rate) surge in M-1 in the second quarter, and perhaps at least some of the 14% increase in the third quarter of 1985 reflected the combined

TABLE 4–6

Interest rates, the money supply, and components

		Federal Funds Rate★ (percent)	M-1	Percentage change at Annual Rate ★★		
				Currency in Circulation	Demand Deposits	Other Checkable Deposits
1982	I	14.68	5.0	6.1	– 3.4	28.6
	II	14.15	3.8	9.5	– 3.4	15.3
	III	10.31	10.6	8.1	3.8	33.6
	IV	8.95	14.8	8.5	8.9	39.0
1983	I	8.77	12.5	11.3	1.2	40.2
	II	8.98	11.4	9.6	5.9	24.9
	III	9.45	8.3	9.1	1.6	20.8
	IV	9.47	5.8	10.5	– .4	12.6
1984	I	9.91	7.0	7.5	3.3	13.1
	II	11.06	7.5	8.2	5.5	10.0
	III	11.30	3.1	6.5	– 2.2	9.2
	IV	8.38	5.1	4.8	1.8	10.7
1985	I	8.58	9.7	6.6	5.3	20.8
	II	7.53	13.4	7.9	14.0	17.4
	III	7.92	14.0	8.3	9.4	27.4
	IV	8.27	8.4	6.9	6.1	13.5

★ Daily average for final month in quarter.

★★ Calculated from last month of each quarter.

Source: Federal Reserve, Board of Governors.

effects of declines in interest rates on alternative money market investments and some special transitory influences. In particular, sharp declines in money market rates (represented in Table 4–6 by the federal funds rate) have, both in late 1982 and late 1984, generally been accompanied within a quarter or two by an acceleration in demand deposit growth and, to a much more striking extent, by growth in other checkable deposits, including interest-bearing NOW accounts. (After a trial period in the Northeast, NOW accounts were introduced nationwide at the beginning of 1981.)

The acceleration in the growth in NOW accounts stemmed largely from the fact that the interest rate spread against alternative money market investments narrowed considerably when money market rates were falling. This situation, in which NOW account rates remained sticky while money market rates plunged, allowed holders of NOW accounts to temporize as to the more desirable place to invest their funds.

The public's precautionary demands for liquid balances may also have given NOW accounts a boost. These demands were fueled in the spring and summer of 1985 by the widely publicized financial problems of state insured savings and loan associations and by the unsettling financial problems of other financial institutions, including the farm credit banks. Nervous depositors may have felt that federally insured NOW accounts provided more convenience, liquidity, and safety than most other short-term investments, while still earning at least a modest return.

Of further note is the fact that growth in the demand deposit component of M-1 soared at a 14% annual rate in the second quarter and a still high 9.4% in the third quarter of 1985. This increase in demand deposits probably reflected three special factors. First, at a time of declining interest rates, there was a need for business depositors to increase their compensating demand balances to pay for bank services. (In all likelihood, this factor was also at work in the sharp 8.9% increase in demand-deposit growth in the final quarter of 1982.) Second, the spurt in demand-deposit growth in the second quarter of 1985 reflected the temporary impact of the bunching of tax refunds owing to IRS computer problems. Third, as alluded to by Fed Chairman Volcker in his July 1985 Humphrey-Hawkins congressional testimony, there was some evidence that brokerage firms were holding more adequate demand balances in the wake of the dramatically publicized questionable cash management practices of a member firm.

The point of this analysis is that Fed watchers need to be aware of the extent to which any surge in M-1 growth is attributable to special influences. If special influences are significant, the monetary authorities will be likely to delay, or at least moderate, any countering reserve-tightening actions. Such reasoning was indicated in the widely quoted Volcker letter of November 6, 1985 (see Appendix III). This significant letter to the Chairman of the House Subcommittee on Domestic Monetary Policy revealed Fed thinking at the November 5 FOMC meeting on a much more timely basis than usual. In the letter, Volcker noted that M-1 growth in the third quarter of 1985 was "well in excess" of the FOMC's rebased target. However he noted that ". . . in light of continued declines in M-1 velocity, growth in the broader monetary aggregates generally within longer-term ranges, and the relatively high foreign exchange value of the dollar, the Committee chose not to move aggressively to tighten reserve availability to constrain M-1 growth." This statement did imply, however, that the Fed took at least some *token* steps in August and September (later confirmed) to tighten reserve pressures in response to the spurt in M-1 growth. Just the same, Volcker strongly suggested in this letter that no further Fed tightening moves were likely. Specifically, he stated that ". . . growth of M-1 over the second half of the year as a whole above the target range established in July would be acceptable."

Special Seasonal Factors

Fed watchers should also be aware of special seasonal influences on weekly M-1 fluctuations. For example, sharp early-month declines in Treasury deposits (not included in M-1) result in a bulge in weekly M-1 balances. This effect is most pronounced when the third day of any month falls on a weekend. The third day of the month is important because it is the day on which massive early-month payments of social security and other government benefits are credited to recipients' money balances. If the third day of the month falls on a Saturday or Sunday, these payments are credited to recipients' money balances on the preceding Friday. This produces a three-day ballooning effect on weekly average money balances.

Money Demand Behavior

If nothing else makes U.S. central banking an art rather than a science, it is the never-ending debate in the academic community over the stability and shape of the public's money demand function. It is ironic that in the mid-1970s writers in the academic literature were puzzling as to why academic money demand functions were *overpredicting* actual money holdings. The study of money demand by Goldfeld, for example, overpredicts, by a whopping $22.3 billion, money demand by the end of a 10-quarter period, starting at the beginning of 1974 and running through the second quarter of 1976.[11] In the mid-1980s, by contrast, estimates of money demand also missed by significant amounts, but in the opposite direction.

Of course, major financial innovations and institutional changes at least partly explain this dichotomy—overpredicting money demand in the mid-1970s and underpredicting it in the mid-1980s. For example, financial innovations in the mid-1970s—such as bank overdraft credit lines, automatic savings account transfer services, and money market mutual funds—all served to reduce the costs of shifting between money balances and alternative interest-bearing money market investments.[12] As a result, the public tended to reduce its holdings of money balances in relation to economic activity, thus increasing money velocity.

Innovations affecting money balance holdings in the 1980s tended to operate in the opposite direction.[13] Specifically, the nationwide introduction of interest-bearing NOW accounts at the beginning of 1981 gave the public a reason to hold M-1 balances for savings as well as transactions purposes. As a result, the public held higher money balances in relation to economic activity, thereby reducing money velocity.

In addition to financial innovations and institutional changes, another important reason for this money demand dichotomy has to do with the public's collective common sense. In the 1970s with inflation soaring to a two-digit pace, money balances lost value faster than virtually any other investment. Real assets like land, paintings, precious metals, commodities—or at least money market investments with two-digit returns—were preferred to M-1 balances. By contrast, money balances have had considerably more appeal in the 1980s, owing to the dramatic decline in inflationary pressures.

These developments for monetary policy imply that Fed policy makers should continue to do what they have been doing from time to time—change their annual monetary targets to adjust for these structural shifts in the public's money demands. This does not imply, however, that the monetary authorities should no longer use money targets for purposes of policy focus and discipline.

How Does the Fed Implement Policy?

For the investor seeking to make a profit in the bond or stock market, an understanding of the means by which the Federal Reserve implements a policy shift in response to undesired fluctuations in money growth may mean the difference between profit or loss. When the Fed tightens reserve pressures, for example, there is an immediate expectation of rising interest rates. As a result, bond and stock market psychology is usually promptly depressed. In order to identify Fed moves to tighten (or ease) bank reserve pressures, it is necessary to understand the nature of Fed open market operations and to examine market factors that can influence bank reserves independently of the Fed.

Chapter 5

Factors Influencing Bank Reserves

The Federal Reserve can do something that no one else in this country can do—it can create high-powered money out of thin air. The Fed can create this high-powered money—or bank reserves—by writing a check on itself in payment for government securities or other assets. Every one dollar of high-powered money that the Fed creates in this way can support several dollars of credit and deposit expansion in the banking system.[1]

But for Fed watchers, this high-powered money multiplication process is *not* where the action is. In the real world, Fed policy shifts involve changes *within* the reserve total affecting *reserve pressures*; the focus should be on the borrowed reserves component of total reserves. Because of the tradition against discount window borrowing and Fed discount window surveillance, an increase in borrowings resulting from Fed efforts to tighten reserve pressures is like putting tension on a spring. With no discount window borrowings, or only frictional levels, there is no tension on the spring. However, when the Fed induces increases in these borrowings, tension rises on the spring—and thus interest rates rise.

Reserve Identity

Perhaps the best way to visualize the role the Fed can play as an influence on the supply of bank reserves is through the reserve identity. This reserve identity can be expressed as follows:

$$\text{Supply of reserves} \atop (NBR + BR) = TR = {\text{Demand for reserves} \atop (ER + RR)}$$

Also: $BR = TR - NBR$

and: $ER = TR - RR$

Another definition:
$$FR = ER - BR$$

Expressed another way:
$$FR = (TR - RR) - (TR - NBR)$$

Subtract TR from each term and thus:
$$FR = NBR - RR$$

where: BR is bank borrowings at the Fed discount window (excluding extended credit).

TR is total reserves.

NBR is nonborrowed reserves (including extended credit).

ER is excess reserves.

RR is required reserves.

FR is free reserves when its sign is positive, or net borrowed reserves when its sign is negative.

On the supply side of this reserve identity, the Fed influences the nonborrowed reserves component (NBR) through its most important policy instrument—open market operations. The Fed can increase nonborrowed reserves (NBR) through its purchase of government securities. The Fed buys (from one or more of the 36 recognized primary dealers in government securities) the government securities by writing a check on itself. The dealer selling these securities to the Fed deposits the Fed's check at its bank—thus adding to the bank's reserves (and to the reserves of the banking system as a whole). The Fed may add permanently to bank reserves through outright purchases of government securities or may add temporarily to bank reserves through System repurchase agreements (RPs). (The System RP calls for the Fed to buy from, for a given period—usually one day—and then sell back to, in a transaction involving one or more of the primary dealers in Government securities, a Fed-determined amount of Government securities at an agreed-upon interest rate.)

When the monetary authorities seek to tighten *reserve pressures* they reduce the growth of the nonborrowed reserves (NBR) component of the reserve identity on the supply side, relative to the growth of the required reserves (RR) component on the demand side. Assuming that the excess reserves (ER) component on the demand side is stable, this forces banks to increase their borrowings at the Fed discount window (BR) to meet their legal reserve requirements.

Role of Borrowed Reserves

At the heart of this reserve-tightening process is the fact that as banks rely increasingly on borrowed reserves (BR) to meet their required-reserve needs they come under increasing strains to promptly repay these borrowed reserves. This is in part due to a reluctance to borrow which is founded on a tradition against bank borrowing at the

Fed discount window. This anti-borrowings "tradition" arises from the perception in financial circles that a bank forced to borrow repeatedly from the Fed could be viewed as financially weak.

Moreover, close Fed surveillance also forces banks to consider these borrowings temporary. The Fed scrutinizes the purpose of such borrowings as well as their frequency and amount. Under Regulation A of the Federal Reserve Act, the Fed dictates that banks may borrow at the discount window only for purposes of: (1) liquidity needs arising from unanticipated loan or deposit activity; (2) the avoidance of overdrafts in reserve accounts; and (3) liquidity needs arising from outside forces such as wire transfer failures. As can be seen in Table 5–1 below, the Fed also establishes specific limitations, according to bank size, on the frequency and amount of borrowings at the discount window.[2] Of course, a bank in trouble may also avail itself of the lender-of-last-resort or "extended credit" facility at the discount window, as Continental Illinois Bank did in a big way (upwards of $6–7 billion) in 1984, and the failing Franklin National Bank did a decade earlier.

Thus, banks borrowing at the discount window must in most cases be prompt to repay these borrowings. This sense of bank urgency in the effort to repay discount window borrowings has been captured by Robert Roosa, a former senior official of the Federal Reserve Bank of New York and the Treasury:

TABLE 5–1

Discount window administration numerical guidelines

Size of Bank	Consecutive weeks Borrowing	Weeks of borrowing within:		Borrowing as a Percent of Domestic Deposits (percent)
		13 Weeks	26 Weeks	
Under $200 million	4–5	6–7	7–8	2.0
$200 million–1 billion	3–4	5–6	7–8	2.0
$1 billion–$3 billion	2–3	4–5	6–7	1.5
More than $3 billion	1–2	3–4	4–5	1.0

Source: Federal Reserve Bank of Cleveland.

"In the American setting, the fact that banks borrow only as a privilege means that even though any individual bank can temporarily, in effect, cause the creation of reserves by borrowing at the discount window, that same bank simultaneously takes on an obligation to find ways of extinguishing those reserves—the more promptly the better—in order to preserve its privilege for use again when unexpected reserve drains occur. Thus, as a general rule, the larger the aggregate volume of bank borrowing from the Federal Reserve, the greater will be the effort then going on, through the banking system, to limit credits and bring reserves into balance with requirements against deposits."[3]

A similar authoritative statement on the restrictive atmosphere surrounding increasing discount window borrowings is that:

"Reserves obtained through borrowing are typically accompanied by a spreading atmosphere of credit restraint, as contrasted with the effect of a corresponding amount of reserves injected by open market operations and appearing in a bank as a normal deposit gain or favorable clearing balance. Administrative restraint exercised by discount officials, together with the reluctance of banks to borrow, makes it likely that a bank forced to borrow will in turn begin to search for federal funds, seek correspondent accommodation, offer securities for sale, sell participations in its more merchantable loans, and/or curtail direct loan activity. Appraisal of the market atmosphere resulting from these developments is one of the important judgements in the formulation of monetary policy.[4]

Banks borrowing temporarily at the Fed discount window must scramble for alternative sources of funds—such as federal funds, RPs, CDs, or Eurodollars. But this scramble for funds by banks seeking to extricate themselves from the discount window in turn exerts upward pressure on the federal funds rate and other market rates. Of course, these alternative sources of funds do not add to the banking system's total supply of reserves.

Market Factors Influencing Bank Reserves

In order for Fed watchers to correctly determine the policy significance of Fed day-to-day open market operations, it is necessary to analyze market factors that influence total reserves independently of Fed actions. In Table 5–2 below, a comprehensive look at sources (including Fed operations) and uses of bank reserves is detailed quarterly for the year 1984.

The Fed watcher should start with a forecast of non-Fed market factors affecting bank reserves. This forecast should be based on historical patterns (see Table 5–3). Start with the pattern of float, for example, in each week of the usually stormy month of December for the past five years. Since there is a strong downtrend in float (which represents Federal Reserve credit extended to banks for checks not collected within the time prescribed by an automatic schedule), it is necessary to place the greatest weight on the float levels in comparable weeks of the immediately preceding years in making the forecast for 1985. Using this historical weekly float data, it is possible to forecast the weekly float pattern for the current year.

This same technique can be used for forecasting the weekly movements in other market factors such as currency in circulation. However, in the case of Treasury deposits at the Fed, additional data on the size of total Treasury cash balances (held at the Fed and in bank Tax and Loan Accounts) as well as on the pattern of the Treasury's new cash financings are required. For example, if the portion of Treasury cash balances held in bank Tax and Loan Accounts pushes much above $21 billion during a quarterly tax payment date, or at other times when Treasury cash coffers are full, then bank give-backs are likely to push Treasury balances at the Fed to unusually high levels. Normally, the Treasury seeks to keep its balances at the Fed stable in a $3–4 billion range. But a surge in total Treasury cash balances could temporarily push Treasury Fed balances in excess of four times this level, thereby absorbing a huge amount of additional bank reserves.

TABLE 5–2
Sources and uses of bank reserves
(millions of dollars)

	December 1983	March 1984	June 1984	September 1984	December 1984	Change December 1983 to Dec. 1984
Starting with:						
Factors supplying reserve funds						
Reserve bank credit outstanding	171,695	168,738	175,397	179,643	183,925	12,230
U.S. government and agency securities	160,352	158,150	163,102	162,811	167,936	7,584
Bought outright	160,163	157,690	161,857	161,025	167,399	7,236
Repurchase agreements	189	460	1,245	1,786	537	348
Loans	745	905	3,166	7,251	3,040	2,295
Float	2,294	1,002	594	462	1,499	–795
Other Federal Reserve assets	8,270	8,667	8,429	9,119	11,450	3,180
Acceptances	34	14	106	0	0	–34
Gold stock	11,123	11,115	11,103	11,096	11,096	–27
Other assets (SDR certificate account)	4,618	4,618	4,618	4,618	4,618	—
Treasury currency outstanding	13,786	15,863	16,082	16,251	16,388	2,602
less:						
Factors absorbing reserve funds						
Deposits with Federal Reserve banks						

TABLE 5-2 [con't]
Sources and uses of bank reserves (millions of dollars)

	December 1983	March 1984	June 1984	September 1984	December 1984	Change December 1983 to Dec. 1984
Treasury	3,591	4,012	3,894	6,117	3,406	–185
Foreign	220	229	244	234	247	27
Other	594	579	439	476	450	–144
Service-related balances and adjustments	1,477	1,940	1,388	1,339	1,676	199
Other Federal Reserve liabilities and capital	5,598	5,705	6,214	6,253	6,370	772
Currency in circulation	168,284	168,317	174,219	176,468	181,720	13,436
Treasury cash holdings	471	488	530	465	511	40
equals:						
Bank reserves with Federal Reserve banks	20,986	19,064	20,272	20,258	21,648	662
plus:						
Bank vault cash	17,908	16,794	17,308	17,897	18,957	1,049
Misc. adjustments	0	418	–62	–117	+99	99
equals:						
Total bank reserves	38,894	36,276	37,518	38,038	40,704	1,810

*Adjustment to compensate for float

Source: Federal Reserve, Board of Governors.

TABLE 5–3
Historical data for float forecasts (typical month)(millions of dollars)

December	Forecast 1985	1984★	1983★	1982★	1981★	1980★
1st week	800	513	1,343	3,357	4,257	5,561
2nd week	1,000	1,833	1,583	3,228	2,864	4,482
3rd week	1,500	1,331	1,655★★	2,347	3,569	4,221★★
4th week	1,200	1,227	3,592★★	3,431	4,016	6,038★★

★ Actual.

★★ Severe storm.

Note: Under the terms of the Monetary Control Act of 1980—which provided for the more efficient processing of checks and under which banks, for the first time, were charged a fee for Fed float credit—there was a dramatic decline in the level of float, beginning in 1981.

Source: Federal Reserve, Board of Governors; Aubrey G. Lanston & Co., Inc.

The volatility in Treasury cash balances can present a significant challenge to the monetary authorities in their day-to-day open market operations. As a case in point, Fed officials faced an unusually large buildup in Treasury balances at the Fed in January, 1986. Reflecting record Treasury sales of SLUGS (special nonmarketable issues) to state and local governments in late 1985, total Treasury balances (both at the Fed and in bank Tax and Loan Accounts) soared to a peak of $42.5 billion on January 22, 1986—approximately double the level usually expected when the Treasury is flush with funds. These state and local governments had borrowed unusually heavily through the issuance of tax-exempt securities in the final quarter of 1985 in order to avoid limitations threatened in 1986 by tax reform legislation; in conformity with arbitrage rules, the bulk of these proceeds from tax-exempt issues were invested in special nonmarketable Treasury issues. As Treasury balances at the Fed alone rose to a high of $19.1 billion (also on January 22), the Fed was forced to meet the resulting reserve drain with an imaginative array of temporary reserve-supplying actions. For example, the Fed initially took the unprecedented step of doing $850 million in 15-day customer RPs. (These customer RPs are normally done for a term of only one day.) Of course, Fed customer RPs reduce the drain on bank reserves that would otherwise have occurred had the customer funds been invested at the Fed in the form of a reverse RP. In addition, the Fed supplied reserves directly through five- and seven-day fixed-term System RPs announced on Wednesday, January 15 for regular delivery by 10:00 A.M. on the following day. Similarly, a week later on Wednesday, January 22, the Fed announced four- and seven-day fixed-term System RPs for regular delivery by 10:00 A.M. on Thursday, January 23.

With this type of forecast of market factors influencing reserves, the Fed watcher can determine the amount of reserves that the Fed must supply to (or drain from) the banking system for defensive purposes—merely to keep reserve pressures unchanged. For example, market factors—consisting of a decline in float and an increase in Treasury balances at the Fed—might be projected to drain $2 billion in reserves from the banking system in the upcoming 2-week bank reserve settlement period.   In response, the Fed must do $2 billion in Fed reserve-adding operations merely to maintain unchanged reserve pressures. It is important to underscore the fact that these reserve projections are highly uncertain and that the Fed may be looking at different numbers based on its own forecast of market factors.

If the Fed failed to add this amount of reserves in this hypothetical two-week bank statement period, this lack of action could have policy significance—the monetary authorities could be in the process of deliberately tolerating a tightening in reserve pressures.

Technical Hints in Analyzing Fed Day-to-Day Actions

Fed watchers must be on guard not to read too much or too little into the monetary authorities' day-to-day open market actions. In seeking to determine whether Fed operations on any given day are aimed merely at offsetting the impact of market factors on bank reserves or whether such operations instead have some policy significance, there are some helpful hints to follow.

1. Don't try to read too much into the "stop-out" rate for Fed RPs. The stop-out rate is merely a product of the amount of reserves the Fed seeks to supply through these RPs relative to the availability of market collateral. Thus, if the Fed has a big adding job to do in order to offset market factors and market collateral happens to be in short supply, the stop-out rate on Fed RPs is likely to decline sharply. But this would in no way signal a Fed policy shift toward ease.

2. Take note of the federal funds rate prevailing at the time of Fed reserve-adding (or draining) actions, but don't read too much into this level. Remember that the Fed Open Market Account Manager may have some idea of the funds rate that *should* be, given the prevailing discount rate level, and assuming that the Fed maintains an unchanged degree of pressure on bank reserve positions; but remember that the Account Manager is not accountable at present for hitting a particular federal funds rate target.

3. Do be sensitive to whether the Fed is "front loading" in supplying reserves early in a period in which an adding job is indicated. Alternatively, the Fed might drain reserves late in a bank statement period in which a draining job is indicated. These actions could mean an easing thrust in Fed policy. Such Fed "front loading" was evident in the second half of May and the first half of June 1985. It was also hinted at in Fed day-to-day operations in mid-November and again in mid-December of the same year.

Chapter 6

Evolution of the
Reserve Control Approach

The Fed's introduction of aggregates into its official FOMC policy directives did not come easily. During the nearly two decades from the 1951 Accord to 1970, the monetary authorities tended to place primary emphasis on money market conditions (typically represented by free reserves or the federal funds rate).

Initially, the Federal Reserve made only a half-hearted attempt to target aggregate growth. In May 1966, for the first time, the FOMC included an aggregate "proviso" clause in its operating directive to the Domestic Manager, System Open Market Account. The proviso clause contained a required reserves aggregate—the first such aggregate given formal recognition in Fed operations.

The May 10, 1966 FOMC directive to the System Account Manager stated in part:

> "To implement this policy, while taking into account the current Treasury financing, System open market operations until the next meeting of the Committee shall be conducted with a view to attaining some further gradual reduction in net reserve availability [free reserves], and a greater reduction *if growth in required reserves does not moderate substantially*." [Italics added.][1]

The final nine words of these operating instructions, in italics for emphasis, represent the proviso clause. After some refinements, FOMC policy makers settled on a bank credit proxy (daily average member bank deposits) as the aggregate included in the proviso clause for the 1966–1970 period. The directive from the September 10, 1968 FOMC meeting, also typical for this period, stated in part:

> "System open market operations until the next meeting of the Committee shall be conducted with a view to maintaining about the prevailing conditions in money and short-term credit markets; provided, however, that operations shall be modified if bank credit appears to be deviating significantly from current projections."

The symbolic gong signalling a new Fed direction was soon to be sounded. In March 1970, a new era was launched as the monetary authorities established a target for money growth—an important reversal in the thrust of the earlier FOMC directives. These earlier directives had placed primary emphasis on money market conditions and only secondary emphasis on aggregates such as bank credit (or the credit proxy). The directive from the March 10, 1970, FOMC meeting finally brought money to the fore, stating in part that:

> "The Committee desires to see moderate growth in money and bank credit over the months ahead. System open market operations until the next meeting of the Committee shall be conducted with a view to maintaining money market conditions [federal funds rate] consistent with that objective."

The main significance of this modification was that henceforth the FOMC would focus its attention on a desired rate of money growth (sometimes with less than complete success).

Federal Funds Rate Targeting Approach

Instead of trying to use direct reserve control techniques to keep actual money growth in line with their new target, the monetary authorities opted for an indirect control approach. Specifically, Fed policy makers sought to keep money growth on its desired course through relatively modest changes in the weekly average federal funds rate. The idea was that if the monetary authorities targeted the funds rate at a higher level, the rates on money market investments would be pushed to higher and more attractive levels, thus causing the public to reduce its demands for non-interest-bearing money balances. Conversely, if the Fed targeted a lower funds rate, downward pressure would be exerted on rates on money market investments, thus increasing the public's demand for money balances.

This Fed technique of money demand control through small changes in a targeted funds rate level was the dominant policy approach through most of the 1970s.[2] The range for allowable adjustments in the funds rate that could be made in response to undesired money fluctuations during the interim between FOMC meetings was initially set at 1¼ percentage points and was moved as wide as 1½ percentage points. Subsequently, the funds rate range was narrowed to only one-half of a percentage point and was typically centered on the funds rate level prevailing at the time of an FOMC meeting. Thus, at this narrowest funds rate target range, no matter how high actual money growth soared above the Fed's desired path, the monetary authorities—except in special cases when, as a result of intermeeting consultations, greater intermeeting leeway was temporarily granted—only had reaction leeway to push the funds rate one-quarter of a percentage point higher.

This rather meek money control technique generally resulted in Fed policy shifts that turned out to be too little and too late. This deficiency was particularly glaring in the second half of the 1970s, when speculative borrowing demands and inflationary psychology were building to a crescendo.

Fed Governor Henry Wallich has observed that Fed efforts to implement its M-1 target by moving the federal funds rate to influence the demand for money:

> " . . . was a perfectly workable technique, but it suffered from a reluctance of the FOMC to move the funds rate fast enough and far enough to keep the money supply on track even over intervals of several months or longer. Because nobody, including the Fed, likes to see interest rates go up, there was over time a bias in policy which allowed the money supply to expand excessively."[3]

This deficiency in money control was not lost on a tall, cigar-smoking gentleman named Paul Volcker when he assumed the Chairmanship of the Federal Reserve Board of Governors in August 1979. The proof of the pudding came shortly with the Fed's "Saturday Massacre" on October 6, 1979.

Automatic Reserve Control Approach

At the special FOMC meeting on October 6, 1979, the monetary authorities, under the guiding hand of Chairman Volcker, decided on a more direct reserve control approach aimed at disciplining money growth. This automatic reserve control approach involved the Fed's establishment of a target path for nonborrowed reserve growth that would meet only the required reserve needs associated with moderate and presumably less inflationary deposit (money) growth. In the event that consumer and business speculative borrowing demands pushed money growth above the Fed's moderate target path, the resulting excessive required reserve demands had to be met by sharply higher bank borrowings at the Fed discount window. If the monetary authorities were not seeing desired results, they could, between FOMC meetings, make further downward adjustments in the target path for nonborrowed reserve growth. These adjustments would in turn cause a surge in discount window borrowings. The result would be a sharp increase in the federal funds rate and in other market rates as banks sought to extricate themselves from the discount window. Higher bank costs of lendable funds would soon be reflected in increases in the prime rate and other rates charged business and consumer borrowers.

In recognition of this prospect, the Fed dramatically widened its target range for the funds rate. The funds rate range was initially widened to four percentage points and then temporarily widened further to as much as $8\frac{1}{2}$ percentage points in 1980 (see Table 6–1).

At the October 6, 1979, FOMC meeting Fed policy makers agreed that:

> "The principal reason advanced for shifting to an operating procedure aimed at controlling the supply of bank reserves more directly was that it would provide greater assurance that the Committee's objectives for monetary growth could be achieved. In the present environment of rapid inflation, estimates of the relationship among interest rates, monetary growth, and economic activity had become less reliable than before, and monetary growth since the first quarter of 1979 had exceeded the rates expected despite substantial increases in short-term rates."[4]

The monetary authorities recognized at the October 6, 1979 FOMC meeting that policy emphasis on directly controlling reserves would result in much greater interest rate volatility.

TABLE 6–1

Federal Reserve policy actions
(August 1979–December 1985)

Date of FOMC Meeting	Type of Fed Policy Action	Bank Adjustment Borrowing at Federal Reserve ★ # (millions of dollars)	Federal Funds Rate # (percent)	Fed Guidelines for Federal Funds Rate (percent)
1979				
August 14	Moderate tightening	1,041	10.64	10¾–11¼
September 18	Moderate tightening	1,268	11.18	11¼–11¾
October 6 +	Major tightening	1,243	11.84	11½–15½
November 20	No change	2,199	14.02	11½–15½
1980				
January 8–9	No change	1,454	13.63	11½–15½
February 4–5	No change	1,252	13.51	11½–15½
February 22 +	Major tightening	1,830	14.38	11½–16½
March 7 +	Major tightening	2,972	16.31	11½–18
March 18	Major easing	3,219	16.35	13–20
April 22	Major easing	2,427	18.42	13–19
May 6 +	Moderate easing	1,997	14.04	10½–19
May 20	Moderate easing	929	10.78	8½–14
July 9	No change	466	9.52	8½–14
August 12	No change	507	9.02	8–14
September 16	Major tightening	840	10.14	8–14
October 21	Moderate tightening	1,412	12.20	9–15
November 18	Moderate tightening	1,841	14.26	13–17
November 26 +	Moderate tightening	2,097	17.43	13–18
December 18–19	No change	1,768	18.95	15–20
1981				
February 2–3	Moderate easing	1,213	19.01	15–20
February 24 +	Moderate easing	1,305	15.77	15–20
March 31	Moderate easing	1,024	14.72	13–18
May 6 +	Major tightening	1,521	16.07	13–18
May 18	Major tightening	1,839	18.55	16–22
July 6–7	Moderate easing	2,122	19.07	15–21
August 18	Moderate easing	1,462	18.51	15–21
October 5–6	Moderate easing	1,165	16.10	12–17
November 17	No change	723	14.52	11–15
December 21–22	No change	325	12.33	10–14
1982				
February 1–2	Major tightening	1,063	13.28	12–16
March 29–30	Moderate easing	1,381	14.68	12–16
May 18	Moderate easing	1,163	14.96	10–15
June 30–July 1	Major easing	1,048	14.06	10–15
August 24	No change	472	11.08	7–11
October 5	Moderate easing	707	10.29	7–10½
November 16	Moderate easing	379	9.51	6–10
December 20–21	No change	368	8.80	6–10

Date of FOMC Meeting	Type of Fed Policy Action	Bank Adjustment Borrowing at Federal Reserve ★ # (millions of dollars)	Federal Funds Rate # (percent)	Fed Guidelines for Federal Funds Rate (percent)
1983				
February 8–9	No change	348	8.77	6–10
March 28–29	No change	426	8.62	6–10
May 24	Moderate tightening	530	8.72	6–10
June 23 +	Moderate tightening	602	8.90	6–10
July 12–13	Moderate tightening	895	9.17	6–10
August 23	No change	944	9.54	6–10
October 4	Moderate easing	971	9.51	6–10
November 14–15	No change	696	9.39	6–10
December 19–20	No change	762	9.43	6–10
1984				
January 30–31	No change	804	9.52	6–10
March 26–27	Major tightening	723	9.74	7½–11½
May 21–22	No change	1,100	10.29	7½–11½
July 16–17	No change	958	11.00	8–12
August 21	No change	1,012	11.54	8–12
October 2 + +	Modest easing	881	11.35	8–12
November 7	Moderate easing	946	9.86	7–11
Dec. 17-18 + +	Modest easing	603	8.92	6–10
1985				
February 12–13++	Modest tightening	419	8.36	6–10
March 26	Modest tightening	553	8.54	6–10
May 21	Modest easing	624	8.23	6–10
July 9–10	No change	611	7.67	6–10
August 20 + +	Modest tightening	498	7.86	6–10
October 1 + +	Modest tightening	615	7.89	6–10
November 4–5	Modest easing	523	8.04	6–10
December 16–17	Modest easing	609 *	8.06	6–10

* Adjustment borrowing total includes seasonal borrowings

Average weekly levels for the interval betweeen the current and preceding FOMC meeting

I Special FOMC meeting

+ + Policy shifts just prior to regular meeting without calling a special meeting

★ Excludes one-day borrowings of $22 billion in the week ended November 27 by a major securities clearing bank experiencing computer problems.

Source: Federal Reserve, Board of Governors, *Record of FOMC Policy Actions;* Aubrey G. Lanston & co., Inc.

"The Committee anticipated that the shift to an operating approach that placed primary emphasis on the volume of reserves would result in both a prompt increase and greater fluctuations in the federal funds rate. It was recognized that on particular days, or for several days, the federal funds rate might rise above or fall below the general limits established and those limits were interpreted to apply to weekly averages. The Committee also agreed that it would consider whether supplementary instructions were needed if it appeared that operations to achieve the necessary restraint in expansion of reserves would tend to maintain the federal funds rate within one percentage point of the upper limit of its range of 11½–15½ percent. It was understood, moreover, that the Committee's decision with respect to open market operations in the period immediately ahead had implications for Federal Reserve Bank discount rates."

The Fed's hope was that the surge in interest rates produced by this automatic reserve control approach would eventually damp business and consumer speculative borrowing demands and help reduce money growth to a less inflationary pace. This reserve control approach eventually proved remarkably successful in disciplining money growth, but it led to wildly volatile and generally high interest rates. The result was a soaring unemployment rate, as the economy was pushed into the deepest recession since the Great Depression.

Although they had achieved a measure of success in producing disciplined monetary growth, Fed policy makers began in late 1982 to back away from the automatic reserve control approach. In its place the Fed established a discretionary reserve control approach. In effect, the monetary authorities reserved the right to override the automatic tightening in reserve pressures and interest rates which had previously accompanied excesses in money growth beyond the Fed's target range.

Perhaps the best internal Fed chronicler of the shift from an automatic reserve control system to a discretionary reserve control system was Fed Governor Wallich. He stated that:

> "Since the fall of 1982, the nonborrowed-reserve strategy and its automaticity have given way to a technique that allows the funds rate to be determined by the market, through the targeting of discount-window borrowing from one reserve-maintenance period to the next, implemented by allowing a flexible nonborrowed-reserves path. At the FOMC meeting an intended borrowing level is set, as a policy decision. This level of borrowing is then deducted from the total of required reserves consistent with the target path for the money supply and an assumed level of excess reserves—in order to derive an initial path for nonborrowed reserves. However, during the intermeeting period, as money and reserve demands deviate from the trajectories set at the time of the FOMC meeting, the intended borrowing level is sought through appropriate adjustments to the initial nonborrowed-reserves path.
>
> The post–fall 1982 procedure differs from the post–October 1979 procedure in that, as anticipated total-reserve demand diverges from initial projections, nonborrowed reserves are adjusted weekly in seeking to achieve a chosen level of borrowed reserves. In contrast, under the October 1979 procedure, borrowing was allowed to change consistent with the attainment of a nonborrowed-reserves path targeted for the entire intermeeting period—although subject to technical adjustments. An assumed level of borrowing under the older procedure was set only initially at the beginning of the inter-FOMC period, but borrowing would subsequently diverge from that initial assumption reflecting unforeseen movements in the demand for money and reserves."[5]

Discretionary Reserve Control Approach

In late 1982 the Fed faced a situation in which Latin American debt problems and concerns over keeping the economy from falling more deeply into recession outweighed the urge to continue to fight inflation. As a result, the Fed began to exercise discretion in adjusting reserve pressures. The Fed would keep reserve pressures unchanged, despite excesses in money growth, depending on certain broader considerations, such as economic performance, inflationary pressures, financial tensions, the U.S. dollar, and, sometimes, the performance of the broader money and credit aggregates. For example, the Fed might maintain unchanged bank reserve pressures despite an overshoot in M-1 growth above its target in a situation in which the economic performance (real GNP) is lagging, inflationary pressures are dormant, the broader aggregates are well-behaved, and the U.S. dollar is excessively strong.

The application of this discretionary reserve control approach in 1985 led the monetary authorities to make no more than minor changes in reserve pressures throughout that year. As a result, federal funds rate volatility was dramatically reduced. Indeed, for most of 1985, funds traded in a relatively tight $7\frac{1}{2}$–$8\frac{1}{2}\%$ range, a far cry from the 1980–1981 period when the funds rate fluctuated from 8% to nearly 20%.

Reflecting the Fed's basically accommodative stance in 1985, M-1 registered a 10.5% increase in the first half of the year, followed by an even more rapid 12.1% increase in the second half of the year. This second-half pace far exceeded the Fed's liberalized target of 3–8% for this period. The Fed was concerned over a weak manufacturing sector pulled down by foreign competition related to a strong dollar and worried about domestic farm credit difficulties and lingering Latin American debt problems. In addition, the Fed was impressed by the absence of renewed inflationary pressures.

The increasing role of the U.S. dollar as a broader consideration influencing Fed policy deliberations was particularly evident in the Fed's discount rate cut from 8% to $7\frac{1}{2}\%$ on May 17, 1985. Fed policy makers were apparently hoping to exert maximum psychological pressure in the direction of lower interest rates to push the excessively strong dollar lower to counter foreign-trade-related weakness in the U.S. farm and manufacturing sectors.

The dollar became a still more important influence on Fed policy on September 22, 1985. At a surprise meeting of the Group of Five (U.S., Britain, France, West Germany, and Japan), the Reagan Administration reversed course and decided to rely in part on coordinated intervention to push the foreign exchange value of the dollar sharply lower, particularly in terms of the Japanese yen. The Group of Five (G-5) initiatives (dubbed the Plaza Agreement in recognition of the New York hotel at which this meeting was held) were based on the reasoning that a lower dollar would eventually cause a reduction in the huge U.S. trade deficit by making U.S. exports less expensive and U.S. imports more expensive, and hopefully calm U.S protectionist emotions. More broadly, the G-5 initiatives were an attempt at closer international fiscal and monetary policy coordination aimed at stepped-up world growth. This coordinated effort to stimulate growth was viewed as the primary means of solving world debt problems.

This coordinated action to push the U.S. dollar lower, along with concerns over debt problems and weak world recovery, virtually eliminated chances of any further Fed tightening moves, despite Fed expectations at the time that U.S. economic activity would gain strength and evidence that M-1 growth remained far above the Fed's 3–8% target for the second half of 1985. Indeed, there was some speculation on the heels of the special G-5 meeting that the Fed might even have to ease reserve pressures or at least reduce the discount rate again in order to assure the success of the official intervention of plan to push the dollar lower. In fact, in the final two months of 1985, the Fed apparently did move to ease reserve pressures sufficiently to fully reverse its small steps to tighten them in August and September.

The zenith of the influence of international considerations on monetary policy may have been reached with the

Fed's cut in the discount rate to 7% from 7½% on March 7, 1986. This Fed move was coordinated, in line with initiatives at the September G-5 meeting, with discount rate cuts started by Germany and Japan on the preceding day. The conditions were perfect for an internationally coordinated cut in interest rates as a sudden plunge in oil prices removed any near-term threat of renewed inflationary pressures.

It goes without saying that the Fed is likely to further revise its reserve control approach as circumstances warrant. U.S. central banking is like the U.S. Constitution in one important respect—its main strength lies in the flexibility of its application to changing circumstances.

Chapter 7

Rules for Fed Watching

Fed watchers should try to get inside the minds of Fed policy makers—to think like they think, to watch the same things that they watch. Some useful rules for Fed Watchers are offered below.

Rule I: *Watch what the Fed watches—not what you think it should watch.*

The biggest mistake some weekly financial letter writers make is trying to impose their own views of what the Fed *should* watch on actual Fed operations. For example, some observers interpret Fed policy shifts solely in terms of the growth of the monetary base or other measures of total reserves. (The monetary base consists of total reserves plus currency in circulation.)

However, as indicated in the preceding chapter, Fed policy intentions are actually focused on two key components within the total reserves measure. For example, when the Fed intends to tighten, it limits nonborrowed reserve growth relative to bank required reserve needs, expecting to force an increase in the borrowed reserves component of total reserves. As banks seek to repay these temporary borrowings at the Fed discount window, they bid up rates on federal funds and other substitute sources of funds. Thus, in order to promptly identify a Fed policy shift, Fed watchers should concentrate (as the Fed does) on the nonborrowed and borrowed reserve components of total reserves, rather than on only the various total reserve measures themselves.

Rule II: *View potential Fed policy shifts as a* reaction *to—rather than a cause of—undesired economic or monetary fluctuations.*

Fed watchers should think of the Fed as a medical doctor (or staff of doctors) and of the economy as the doctor's "patient." When the "patient" becomes hyperactive—as reflected in excessive quarterly real GNP growth and undesirably high money growth—the Fed "doctor" can be expected to *respond* by administering a "tranquilizer" in the form of a dose of reserve restraint. Conversely, if the "patient" falls into a state of depression, the Fed "doctor" is likely to *react* by administering a "stimulant" in the form of a dose of ease.

Fed watchers should remember that the Fed *responds* to undesired fluctuations in economic activity or money growth. The Fed watcher who is aware of this fact can avoid the gross blunder often made by doctrinaire monetarists. These misguided zealots assume that if, for example, money growth has been excessive over the past month or two, the Fed intended it to be so and therefore the Fed is bent on easing policy and pushing interest rates lower. But the harsh reality is exactly the opposite. The monetary authorities are likely to be as shocked as anyone else over higher-than-targeted money growth. Thus, under normal circumstances, the Fed's response to excessive money growth will be to tighten reserve pressures and to push rates higher.

Rule III: *Try to anticipate the next fed policy shift—not explain the last one.*

Fed watchers should devote most of their energies to collecting data concerning current or prospective near-term fluctuations in quarterly real GNP growth, monthly M-1 growth, and market factors influencing weekly bank reserve availability. To aid in projecting real GNP growth in particular, at least six key monthly series are important: nonfarm payroll employment, personal consumption expenditures, housing starts, industrial production, new orders for durable goods (including the important component, new orders for nondefense capital goods), and factory (durable and nondurable) order backlogs. Backlogs are defined as factory new orders less shipments. Fed watchers should keep an eye on these series for the preceding six months or so and take note when three or more of these series show a pattern of significant and sustained advance (or decline).

Fed watchers who use this approach are in a better position to anticipate the next Fed policy shift. After all, at any given time, this "next" Fed policy shift is the one being discounted in the bond and stock markets.

Of course, Fed watchers should do enough homework on recent Fed policy shifts to determine the Fed's prevailing reserve control approach—i.e., whether the Fed is targeting the federal funds rate, using an automatic reserve control approach, or perhaps targeting discount window borrowings on a discretionary basis. Moreover, the policy records of Fed FOMC meetings and Fed officials' speeches should be examined closely in order to be familiar with the major broader considerations dominating Fed thinking at a given time. For example, Fed policy makers might consider it appropriate to delay a tightening response to excessive M-1 growth in light of rising financial tensions. These tensions could range from the threatened failure of a large bank to depositor runs on privately insured savings and loan associations, or from domestic farm credit problems to a flare-up of problems with bank loans to less-developed countries.

Rule IV: *Pay attention to what the Fed does—not to what it says.*

This rule is less applicable to Fed policy under the leadership of Chairman Volcker than to policy under his immediate predecessors. Indeed, one of the strong points of Chairman Volcker's policy approach is that as a rule he does what he says.

The proof of the consistency between Fed talk and action under Volcker can be found in his semiannual Humphrey-Hawkins testimony before Congress. In his July 1985 testimony, Chairman Volcker stated that the Fed had moved to liberalize the Fed's target for M-1 growth in the second half of 1985 because it would have been inappropriate to tighten reserve pressures at that time, as would have been required if the Fed had adhered to the old, more restrictive target. At the same time, Chairman Volcker implied that, in view of an unexpected May–June surge in M-1 growth and a sharp plunge in the value of the U.S. dollar in the foreign exchange markets, it would have been inappropriate for the Fed to ease reserve pressures further. In fact, at the July 9–10, 1985, FOMC meeting, Chairman Volcker and other Fed policy makers indicated that, although they anticipated an unchanged policy stance in the period immediately following the meeting, future policy shifts would more likely be in the direction of restraint than ease. In line with this restrictive leaning, the Fed made modest moves to tighten bank reserve pressures both in early August (see the analysis of the August 20 FOMC meeting minutes in Appendix IV) and in early September of that year.

In earlier February 1984 congressional testimony Fed Chairman Volcker had implied that the Fed might have to tighten reserve pressures further to guard against a renewal of inflationary pressures. Again, true to Volcker's word, at its March 26–27 FOMC meeting, the Fed decided to tighten reserve pressures in response to a 1984 first-quarter surge in real GNP growth and excessive monetary growth.

By contrast, historical evidence is ample that Fed leaders have often said one thing and done another. For example, in the period from 1975 to early 1978 under Fed Chairman Burns, and again in most of 1978 and early 1979 under Fed Chairman Miller, the Fed talked of restrictive action, but was averse to biting the proverbial restrictive bullet. This gap between Fed restrictive talk and action was never greater than under Miller's less-than-forceful leadership, when Fed reserve-tightening moves were generally too timid to have a discernible effect on the surging speculative borrowing demands and rampant inflation psychology that prevailed at the time.

Looking ahead, Fed watchers should be aware that Volcker's successor may develop another gap between Fed talk and performance, especially concerning the fight against inflation. Indeed, the monetary authorities may get caught in an increasingly strident debate within their own policy circles, pitting the *practical* monetarists (including disciples of Fed Chairman Volcker) who favor at least some monetary discipline and moderate economic growth against the potentially divisive band of Reagan Administration-appointed Governors (Martin—subsequently replaced by Heller, Seger, Johnson, and Angell), who tend to favor monetary ease and relatively rapid growth.[1] In fact, in January 1986, just prior to the confirmation of Reagan nominees Johnson and Angell, such a split may have been indicated by the Fed Board of Governors close 3–2 vote (Martin and Seger dissenting) favoring tighter margin requirements on corporate high-risk "junk" bonds issued in connection with merger or takeover attempts. Even more ominously, the four Reagan appointees banded together for the first time as a Board of Governors majority and outvoted Fed Chairman Volcker and two other dissenting Governors in a key policy action in late February 1986. Indeed the financial markets were shaken by a leak of news from within the walls of the Federal Reserve (around mid-March) that there had been for all intents and purposes a most unusual "palace coup" attempt apparently led by Preston Martin, Vice Chairman of the Board of Governors. Specifically, the Reagan appointees prevailed in an initial 4–3 vote on February 24 favoring a discount rate cut to 7% from 7½%.[2] An angry Chairman Volcker was, however, apparently able to get Governor Angell to change his vote within hours of this vote (before it could be announced) thereby allowing the discount rate cut to be deferred until March 7 when it could be coordinated with German and Japanese discount rate cuts. This was done in order to minimize the negative impact of a U.S. discount rate cut on the dollar.

A befitting climax to this strange tale of "palace intrigue" came suddenly on March 21, 1986 when Vice Chairman Martin at a hastily called press conference announced his resignation. Martin, who throughout his term on the Board of Governors had been unable to hide his ambition to be Fed Chairman, insisted that he was resigning because the White House could not promise him that he would be named Fed Chairman at the end of Volcker's second term in August, 1987. However, there is every reason to suspect that the sorry (palace coup) episode at least indirectly hastened Martin's departure. In the case of a major internal split, the Fed may be frozen into a position of all talk and no action, or perhaps could be pushed toward an easy-money policy bias.

Another more immediate possible outcome is that the Fed may lack anti-inflation resolve if the monetary authorities try to watch "everything" (i.e., domestic debt difficulties, the farm crisis, energy sector problems, international debt problems, the dollar, etc.) rather than focus on one or two key monetary or economic signals. The October 1, 1985, FOMC policy record hinted that the Fed might be moving dangerously close to this "watch everything" approach. Specifically, the discussion of near-term policy implementation noted that, "Currently sensitive conditions in domestic and international financial markets and debt problems in some sectors of the economy such as agriculture were themselves a restraining force on the economy and argued against a policy course that might entail appreciably higher interest rates in the short run."

Section III

Indicators of Fed Policy Shifts

To be successful, a Fed watcher must promptly identify Fed policy shifts. In this way, he or she can get a leg up on profitable trading opportunities in the bond and stock markets. To assist in identifying policy shifts, a third item is needed in the Fed watcher's practical "tool kit"—in addition to quarterly real GNP growth and monthly M-1 growth. This important item is bank borrowings at the Fed discount window (excluding extended credit). It is the most sensitive, if not always perfectly accurate, indicator of Fed policy shifts. The weekly borrowings figure is reported in the Fed's statistics each Thursday at 4:30 P.M. eastern standard time and is published each Friday morning in the *Wall Street Journal* and other newspapers. No single financial statistic is more important to participants in the bond and stock markets.

Chapter 8

The All-Powerful Discount Window Borrowings Signal

When the Federal Reserve System was in its infancy (it was established in 1913), the discount window reigned supreme as the Fed's major policy instrument. Under the commercial loan theory of credit or the so-called "real bills"[1] doctrine which dominated thinking at the time, banks could present for credit at the Fed discount window notes of indebtedness or "bills" representing bank loans made to businesses for purposes of raising working capital to produce or distribute goods and services. In effect, each "good" was viewed as being produced with a "real bills" ribbon tied around its "neck"; when the "good" was sold, the proceeds could be used to untie the ribbon and repay the loan. This approach was thought to make the supply of credit sufficiently elastic to support expanding real business opportunities. The hope was that tying credit expansion so closely to the ebb and flow of real economic activity lessened the chance of a buildup in speculative activities and of potential inflationary pressures.

To be sure, this "real bills' concept had flaws. The credit extended through the Fed discount window represented, of course, high-powered money or reserves which could support a multiple expansion in bank credit and deposits. Moreover, there was no way to determine whether the uses to which this credit was put were productive or nonproductive.[2] The fact that Reserve Banks were permitted, under a 1916 amendment to the Federal Reserve Act, to make advances to banks on their own promissory notes secured by the pledge of government securities also served to loosen the link between real economic activity and discount window advances.

Nevertheless, the central role of the discount window as a source of reserves to support bank credit and deposit expansion prevailed until the early 1920s when another Fed policy instrument—open market operations—was accidentally discovered. Fed officials discovered the reserve-supplying potential of open market operations as a by-product of efforts by various district Federal Reserve Banks to beef up their holdings of securities in order to earn interest to use to pay increasing operating expenses.

Reserve Position Doctrine

Even after Fed open market operations had displaced the discount window as the Fed's primary policy instrument, the discount window continued to play an important policy role. According to the reserve position doctrine (best articulated by a bright senior member of the Fed Board's research staff—Winfield Riefler), bank borrowings at the Fed discount window represented only a temporary "relief valve" for banks that were hard-pressed for funds. For example, when the monetary authorities were seeking to tighten bank reserve pressures through open market sales of securities, banks were expected to fall back on the discount window for funds as a safety cushion.[3]

But, as Riefler reasoned, banks had an ingrained tradition against borrowing from the Fed because such borrowings were generally seen as a sign of financial weakness. Thus, banks that were forced to turn temporarily to the discount window for funds were quick to extricate themselves by seeking alternative sources of funds such as could be found in the federal funds market. This scramble for funds, as banks attempted to end their reliance on the discount window, tended to exert upward pressure on the federal funds rate and on rates on other bank sources of lendable funds as well. This reasoning led Riefler to discover a positive statistical correlation between bank borrowings at the Fed and money market rates.

Modern Borrowings Doctrine

In today's setting, Fed watchers should closely follow bank borrowings at the Fed discount window for two major reasons. First, when the monetary authorities decide to tighten reserve pressures they increase their operating target for such borrowings. By this primary means the FOMC communicates a policy decision to the Domestic Manager of the System Open Market Account, who must implement this decision. In a nutshell, the extent of a Fed tightening move is best identified and defined in terms of the size of the increase in discount window borrowings. Thus, a *modest* Fed tightening move is signalled by an increase of approximately $50–150 million in bank borrowings at the Fed discount window (excluding extended credit), measured as the change in the average level of such borrowings in successive two-week bank reserve settlement periods. Such an increase in bank reserve pressures might push the federal funds rate one-quarter of a percentage point higher. A *moderate* Fed tightening move would be reflected in a $200–350 increase in such borrowings. Such a tightening in reserve pressures might lift the federal funds rate one-half point. A *fairly strong* Fed tightening move would be signalled by a larger—$400–550 million—increase in borrowings. This increase in reserve pressures might push the federal funds rate a full percentage point higher. Finally, an *aggressively large* (major) Fed tightening move would be signalled by a hefty increase of $800 million or more in borrowings. This tightening of reserve pressures might result in a spurt of the federal funds rate of two percentage points or more.

A second reason for following fluctuations in bank borrowings at the Fed discount window is that a significant increase in these borrowings, following the pattern that Riefler discovered earlier, will almost instantly be reflected (as suggested above) in upward pressures on the federal funds rate, as was seen during periods of Fed tightening moves in 1966, 1969, 1973–1974, 1979–early 1980, 1981–early 1982, and early 1984 (note Charts 8–1 and 8–2).

In some recent years, the monetary authorities have changed their borrowings target frequently. Note in Table 8–1 below that in 1984, for example, the Fed changed its borrowings target no less than nine times, and by as little as $50 million. During that year, the Fed decided in late March on a significant move to tighten reserve pressures in response to a surge in first-quarter real GNP growth and excessive money growth. Later in the same year, the Fed engaged in a series of moves to ease bank reserve pressures in response to a pronounced slowing in economic activity and money growth.[4] In 1985, the Fed adjusted its policy stance eight times. However, the Fed's adjustments in reserve pressure were much more timid than in 1984, as indicated by the fact that the Fed kept its borrowing target within a relatively tight $300–$500-million range in 1985.

Table 8–1 contains an important clue for Fed watchers seeking to promptly identify Fed policy shifts. Note that Fed changes in its borrowings target are almost immediately reflected in changes in actual borrowings. Speci-

CHART 8-1
Discount rate and Federal funds rate (monthly 1965–1985)

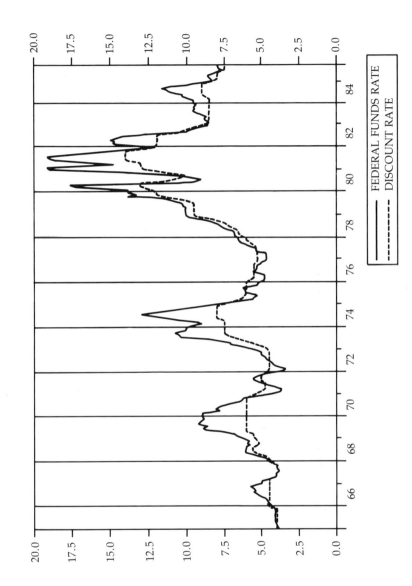

FEDERAL FUNDS RATE
DISCOUNT RATE

CHART 8-2

Bank discount window borrowings from the Federal Reserve (monthly 1965–1985)

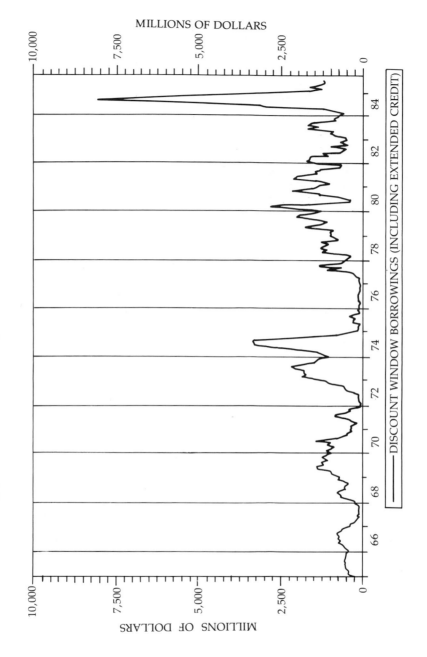

MILLIONS OF DOLLARS

DISCOUNT WINDOW BORROWINGS (INCLUDING EXTENDED CREDIT)

TABLE 8–1

Federal Reserve borrowings targets and actual borrowings in 1984
(millions of dollars)

FOMC Meeting Date	Fed Borrowings Target††	Bank Statement Date	Actual Borrowings
1983			
December 19–20	650	December 21	842
1984			
		January 4	1,022
		January 18	674
January 30	650	February 1	591
		February 15	553
		February 29	564
		March 14	668
March 26–27	1,000	March 28	1,106
		April 11	1,277
		April 25	1,188
May 21–22	1,000	May 9	1,003
		May 23	932
		June 6	1,033
		June 20	991
		July 4	1,064
July 16–17	1,000	July 18	744
		August 1	1,057
		August 15	1,012
August 21	1,000	August 29	962
(September 12)	(900)	September 12	754
(September 26)	(850)	September 26	741
October 2	750	October 10	1,018
(October 26)e	(700)	October 24	803
November 7	575	November 7	1,190
		November 21	588
(December 5)	(500)	December 5	763
(December 13)e	(400)	December 19	457
December 17	300	January 2	653

*Includes a special allowance of an additional $50 million for discount window borrowings of state-insured savings and loan associations in Ohio and Maryland.

†Includes a record $21 billion in discount window borrowings on November 21 by a major securities clearing New York City bank experiencing computer problems.

††Bank adjustment plus seasonal borrowings at the Federal Reserve, excluding extended credit.

( ) Fed borrowings targets established between FOMC meetings.

Note: Actual borrowings are two-week averages corresponding with bank two-week statement periods.

e Estimated.

Source: "Monetary Policy and Open Market Operations in 1984," Federal Reserve Bank of New York, *Quarterly Review*, Spring 1985.

TABLE 8–1 [con't]
Federal Reserve borrowings targets and actual borrowings in 1984
(millions of dollars)

FOMC Meeting Date	Fed Borrowings Target	Bank Statement Date	Actual Borrowings
1985			
		January 2	653
		January 16	260
(January 30)	(350)e	January 30	383
February 12-13	350	February 13	381
		February 27	569
		March 13	641
March 26	400	March 27	451
		April 10	481
		April 24	392
(May 8)	(450)*	May 8	557
May 21	350	May 22	1,065
		June 5	604
		June 19	511
		July 3	547
July 9-10	350	July 17	801
		July 31	411
(August 14)	(400)	August 14	481
August 20	425	August 28	478
(September 11)	(500)	September 11	723
		September 25	515
October 1	500	October 9	768
		October 23	470
November 4-5	450	November 6	477
		November 20	657
		December 4	2,425†
December 16-17	350	December 18	316

fically, in line with its intentions to tighten reserve pressures, the Fed moved in late March to increase its borrowings target from $650 million to $1 billion. In the two-week bank statement period ended March 28, this Fed tightening move was reflected as an increase in actual borrowings to $1.1 billion from $668 million in the immediately preceding period. Similarly, in line with its easing intentions, the Fed reduced its borrowings target from $1 billion at the August 21 FOMC meeting to $750 million at the October 2 FOMC meeting (with two smaller easing steps in between). This Fed easing move was accompanied by a decline in actual borrowings to $741 million for the two-week bank statement period ended September 26 from $1.0 billion in the two-week bank statement period ended August 15.

Evaluating Volatility in Discount Window Borrowings

One note of caution is in order for Fed watchers using the borrowings figure as an indicator of Fed policy shifts. Actual borrowings, as demonstrated in Table 8–1, are prompt to adjust to Fed changes in its borrowings target. However, once the Fed has established a new borrowings target, the actual level of borrowings for a given two-week bank settlement period may deviate significantly from the Fed's target level. For example, during some statement periods an unexpected surge may occur in bank demand for excess reserves (as often happens around year-end or mid-year bank statement periods or perhaps during periods of financial uncertainty when bank demands for excess reserves increase for precautionary reasons). Sometimes these spurts in bank demands are met, on the reserve supply side, by an increase in borrowings. In this case, free reserves (excess reserves less borrowings) would serve as a better indicator of Fed policy intentions than borrowings alone. Alternatively, should the Fed become aware of such a sudden increase in bank demand for excess reserves and meet it by supplying extra nonborrowed reserves through open market operations (as was apparently done in January 1986), then discount window borrowings would remain the appropriate indicator of Fed policy intentions.

Yet another instance when actual borrowings may stray from the Fed's target level in statement periods could occur when the monetary authorities make large errors in their forecast of market factors influencing bank reserve availability. Such borrowings volatility is evident in the worksheet reproduced in Table 8–2. Finally, unusual

TABLE 8–2
Selected Fed policy indicators (millions of dollars)

1985	Fed Funds (rate percent)	Free Reserves 1 Week	Free Reserves 2-Week Avg.	Discount Window Borrowings 1 Wk	Discount Window Borrowings 2-Wk Avg.	Excess Reserves 1 Week	Excess Reserves 2-Week Avg.	Ratio Borr./Tot. Res.	Nonborrowed Reserves 1 Week	Nonborrowed Reserves 2-Week Growth (% change)	Required Reserves 1 Week	Required Reserves 2-Week Growth (% change)	M-1 w/e:	M-1 (billions of dollars)
Jan 2	8.75	-1734	558	1136	653	-598	1211	(1.7)	38,800	(+2.6)	38,246	(+1.3)	Dec. 31	557.4
9	8.27	743		245		988							Jan 7	562.1
16	8.23	5	374	275	260	280	634	(.7)	39,564	(+2.0)	39,190	(+2.5)	14	560.2
23	8.19	242		243		480							21	563.4
30	8.45	532	387	523	383	1055	770	(1.0)	39,211	(-.9)	38,823	(-.9)	28	563.4
Feb 6	8.59	943		402		1345							Feb. 4	564.9
13	8.44	318	630	360	381	678	1011	(.9)	39,962	(+1.9)	39,331	(+1.3)	11	567.3
20	8.57	-201		460		259							18	569.0
27	8.40	686	242	678	569	1364	811	(1.4)	39,803	(-.4)	39,563	(+.6)	25	572.8
Mar 6	8.63	1602		419		2021							Mar. 4	572.7
13	8.52	-1321	140	862	641	-459	781	(1.6)	39,915	(+.3)	39,773	(.5)	11	570.9
20	8.75	493		519		1012							18	570.1
27	8.38	221	357	382	451	603	808	(1.1)	40,199	(+.7)	39,840	(+.2)	25	572.9
Apr 3	8.68	1043		386		1429							Apr. 1	575.0
10	8.45	-890	76	575	481	-315	557	(1.2)	39,830	(-.9)	39,753	(-.2)	8	574.0
17	8.46	1520		335		1855							15	573.7
24	7.69	-541	490	449	392	-92	882	(.9)	40,957	(+2.8)	40,466	(+1.8)	22	576.4
May 1	8.35	-1385		600		-785							29	575.5
8	8.19	-1674	145	515	557	2189	702	(1.4)	40,214	(-1.8)	40,072	(-1.0)	May 6	577.7
15	8.14	-699		839		140							13	577.9
22	7.91	285	207	1291	1065	1579	858	(2.7)	40,404	(+.5)	40,617	(+1.4)	20	582.3
29	7.60	-371		487		116							27	585.0

Month	Day													Month	Day	
June	5	7.75	806	218	721	604	1527	822	(1.5)	40,981	(+1.4)	40,762	(+.4)	Jan.	3	586.0
	12	7.62	935		402		1337								10	591.0
	19	7.13	-513	211	620	511	107	722	(1.2)	41,490	(+1.2)	41,277	(+1.3)		17	589.6
	26	7.46	355		242		598								24	592.2
July	3	8.06	913	634	851	547	1764	1181	(1.3)	42,124	(+1.5)	41,299	(+.5)	Jul.	1	596.1
	10	8.07	-1600		953		-647								8	596.6
	17	7.77	1379	111	648	801	2027	690	(1.9)	41,700	(-1.0)	41,810	(+.7)		15	591.8
	24	7.88	904		418		1322								22	595.5
	31	7.64	172	538	404	411	576	949	(1.0)	42,288	(+1.4)	41,746	(+.1)		29	596.8
Aug	7	7.92	277		345		522							Aug	5	602.1
	14	7.88	363	270	617	481	980	751	(1.1)	42,515	(+.5)	42,258	(+1.2)		12	603.1
	21	8.06	-314		555		241								19	605.8
	28	7.78	1298	491	400	478	1698	969	(1.1)	42,898	(+.8)	42,405	(+.3)		26	608.3
Sept	4	7.88	344		1024		1368							Sept	2	609.5
	11	7.80	-446	-51	422	723	-24	672	(1.7)	42,644	(-.6)	42,695	(+.6)		9	613.7
	18	7.85	-443		421		-27								16	610.2
	25	7.96	752	152	608	515	1360	667	(1.2)	43,066	(+1.0)	42,914	(+.5)		23	609.6
															30	614.8
Oct	2	8.12	197	-121	816	768	1073	647	(1.8)	42,841	(-.5)	42,962	(.1)	Oct.	7	612.1
	9	7.84	-440		720		280								14	605.6
	16	8.03	-345		305		-40								21	613.9
	23	8.14	1015	335	634	470	1650	805	(1.1)	43,105	(+.6)	42,782	(-.4)		28	611.5
	30	7.89	523		357		885							Nov	4	612.1
Nov	6	8.30	140	334	597	477	737	811	(1.1)	43,354	(+.6)	43,028	(+.6)		11	613.7
	13	7.95	1649		258		1907								18	616.6
	20	8.13	-1159	244	1055	657	-104	902	(1.5)	43,468	(+.3)	43,231	(+.5)		25	621.0
	27	7.71	-1827		3767		1940							Dec.	2	626.4
Dec	4	8.49	-945	-1387	1083	2425	137	1038	(5.4)	42,632	(-1.9)	44,005	(+1.8)		9	623.3
	11	8.03	723		163		886								16	622.5
	18	8.05	299	510	468	316	767	826	(.7)	44,398	(+4.1)	43,885	(-.3)			

Source: Federal Reserve, Board of Governors, Aubrey G. Lanston & Co., Inc.

week-to-week volatility in borrowings may result when the Fed serves as a lender-of-last-resort to banks or other financial institutions in trouble for periods too short, or amounts too small, to be classified as extended credit.

When Fed watchers are uncertain about whether volatility in discount window borrowings reflects Fed policy shifts or merely technical factors, they might try averaging the adjustment and seasonal borrowings figures over longer intervals. For example, it might be useful to compare average borrowings over the five- to six-week intervals between FOMC meetings. Thus, if the average discount window borrowings level over the five- to six-week period preceding a FOMC meeting happened to be significantly higher than the average borrowings level over the five- to six-week period succeeding that meeting, then a Fed move at the meeting to ease reserve pressures is a strong possibility. Also, two computations in Table 8–2 may be helpful. If the Fed's intentions are to maintain a stable policy stance, the *ratio* of adjustment (and seasonal) borrowings to total reserves should, barring major wire breakdowns or large reserve forecasting errors, remain relatively stable (i.e., not change on a sustained basis by more than .2). Also, the two-week growth rate in nonborrowed reserves plus extended credit should, with Fed efforts to maintain unchanged reserve pressures, remain fairly closely in line with the two-week growth rate in required reserves (i.e., not deviate on a sustained basis by more than 1–2%).

Chapter 9

The Federal Funds Rate—
An Unheralded Market Beacon

The federal funds rate (the rate on reserves held on account at the Fed that are loaned and borrowed among banks usually, but not exclusively, overnight) is an obscure but highly significant money market indicator. Movements in this highly sensitive funds rate foreshadow movements in other market rates, such as the prime rate, that are more directly relevant to borrower well-being.

Linchpin Role

The federal funds rate is important to the Fed watcher because this rate serves as the linchpin linking Fed policy shifts to bond yields and stock prices and ultimately to fluctuations in economic activity. The relationships between the funds rate, bond yields, and stock prices can be seen in Charts 9–1 and 9–2 below.

CHART 9-1
Federal funds rate and bond yield

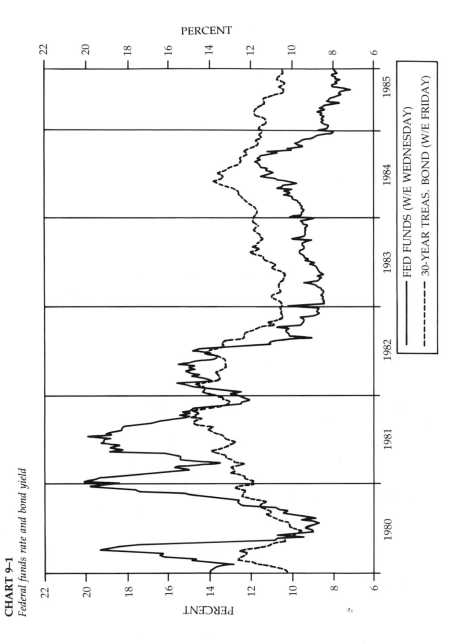

FED FUNDS (W/E WEDNESDAY)
30-YEAR TREAS. BOND (W/E FRIDAY)

CHART 9–2
Stock prices

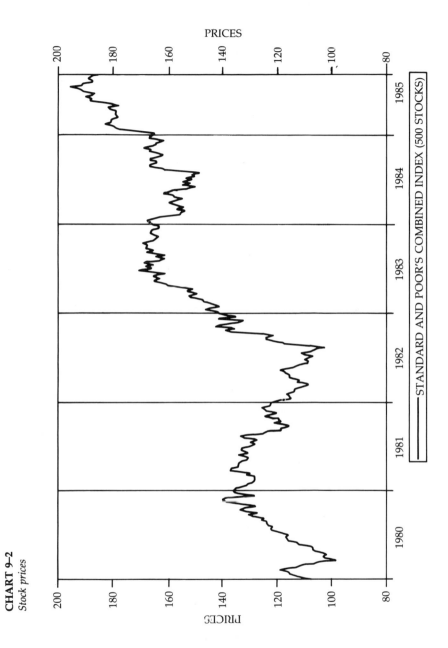

PRICES

STANDARD AND POOR'S COMBINED INDEX (500 STOCKS)

200 180 160 140 120 100 80

1980 1981 1982 1983 1984 1985

103

Although the monetary authorities have not targeted the funds rate, per se, since late 1979 when the funds-rate-targeting approach to money control was discarded (see Chapter 6), in its current policy implementation process, the Fed uses the funds rate as a key indicator of money market pressures. For example, in bank statement periods when the Fed has overestimated bank reserve availability, the Fed will typically interpret a firming funds rate as a signal that it should add more reserves through open market operations than originally contemplated. Similarly, Fed policy makers may at times react to a rising funds rate by temporarily adding reserves through open market operations, even if no bank reserve needs are immediately indicated. However, Fed countering moves to drain an equal amount of reserves through reverse RPs can be expected later in the same bank statement period. On such occasions, the motive of the monetary authorities has been to convince market participants that a Fed move to tighten reserve pressures was not contemplated.

The close relationship between Fed-induced changes in the federal funds rate and bond yields can be seen in Chart 9–1. Moreover, it would appear that stock prices often tend to dance to the tune of the federal funds rate and bond yields (as highlighted in Chart 9–2).

As a case in point, an aggressive series of Fed moves to ease bank reserve pressures were made at a time of credit controls and sudden economic weakness in the spring of 1980. These Fed easing moves in turn, were associated with sharp declines in the funds rate and in bond yields, and promptly followed by a brisk rally in stock prices.

By contrast, the period from the fall of 1980 through early 1982 saw recurrent Fed moves to tighten reserve pressures. Accordingly, the funds rate and bond yields surged higher in the fall of 1980, the spring of 1981, and again to a lesser extent at the beginning of 1982. The stock market could not buck this climb in interest rates, and stock prices trended downward.

The classic conditions for a sharp decline in bond yields and a stock market rally occurred in the summer and fall of 1982. To the surprise of almost everyone, the Fed began to ease reserve pressures aggressively over this period because of concern over a deepening recession. The funds rate plunged. Stock market participants concluded that lower rates not only improved the competitiveness of stocks relative to money market instruments and bonds, but also would eventually stimulate economic activity and profits.

The Fed turned around and tightened reserve pressures again in May 1983 and in March 1984. As a result, the funds rate and bond yields moved higher and the stock market rally faltered.

The Fed reversed course yet again in late 1984 when, against the background of weakening economic activity and slowing monetary growth, it moved to ease reserve pressures. The resulting declines in the funds rate and bond yields set the stage for another stock market rally. Contrary to the usual pattern, the decline in bond yields slightly preceded the decline in the funds rate in mid-1984. Apparently, the anti-inflation psychology created by the Fed's earlier tightening moves in May 1983 and March 1984 was beginning to take hold in the bond market. More immediately, it was weaker-than-expected increases in producer prices, particularly in May and June of 1984, that helped drive home to investors the point that inflationary pressures were on the wane. A similar "watershed" change in inflationary psychology occurred in early 1986, as investors sharply reduced their inflationary expectations in the wake of a surprisingly sharp plunge in oil prices.

The overwhelming power of the mere expectation of Fed easing moves (including a possible discount rate cut), quite apart from the realities of the Fed's actual policy stance, was vividly demonstrated in the closing months of 1985. Largely based on only the belief that a major Fed easing move (including a possible discount rate cut) was in the cards, bond yields plummeted in November and December 1985, and stock prices skyrocketed. In fact, there was only a modest Fed easing in reserve pressures and no discount rate cut in December 1985.

Historical Development

The federal funds market began to develop in the early 1920s at about the time that Fed open market operations were discovered.[1] Banks with surplus reserves (usually smaller banks) began to loan funds to banks facing a deficit in reserves (usually larger banks). As the funds market blossomed, both bank and nonbank funds brokers became the middlemen, matching borrowers and lenders of funds.

Trading activity in the funds market picked up sharply in the late 1920s but then subsided in the depression-plagued 1930s when the banking system was awash in excess reserves. Activity remained depressed during the war years of the 1940s and until the Treasury–Federal Reserve Accord of 1951. During this period, the Fed created enough money to finance an avalanche of federal debt at pegged interest rates, leaving the banking system with a mountain of liquidity.

The funds market was given a renewed lease on life in the mid-1960s when Morgan Guaranty Bank broke the convention under which the funds rate had never exceeded the Fed discount rate. This freed the funds rate to more accurately reflect the availability of reserves, and the volume of funds-trading activity has been rising ever since.

As can be seen in Table 9–1, bank liability management techniques truly came of age in the tight-money environment of 1969.[2] As banks scrambled for funds to meet business and consumer credit demands, they sharply increased their borrowings (mainly consisting of federal funds and RP borrowings) from $8.9 billion in 1968 to

TABLE 9-1

Selected short-term commercial bank sources of funds ★
(millions of dollars)

Year	Borrowings	Year	Borrowings
1921	698	1950	90
1922	370	1951	34
1923	575	1952	188
1924	154	1953	62
1925	555	1954	31
1926	511	1955	159
1927	463	1956	75
1928	918	1957	77
1929	405	1958	73
		1959	615
1930	89		
1931	685	1960	163
1932	67	1961	471
1933	24	1962	3,627
1934	2	1963	3,664
1935	1	1964	2,679
1936	23	1965	4,472
1937	9	1966	4,859
1938	1	1967	5,777
1939	3	1968	8,899
		1969	18,360
1940	3		
1941	23	1970	19,375
1942	13	1971	25,912
1943	49	1972	38,083
1944	123	1973	68,800
1945	219	1974	78,300
1946	45	1975	70,600
1947	65	1976	99,600
1948	56	1977	117,700
1949	20	1978	154,700
		1979	180,200
		1980	211,000
		1981	250,800
		1982	278,300
		1983	275,100
		1984	304,600
		1985	361,500

★Includes Federal funds borrowings, RP borrowings, and borrowings at the Fed discount window.

Source: Federal Reserve, Board of Governors.

$18.4 billion in 1969. Clearly, banks were relying increasingly on liability funds sources to support lending activities, rather than on the more traditional sales of liquid assets such as short-term government securities. The explosive growth of these borrowings continued in the 1970s and 1980s, reaching a whopping $361.5 billion by the end of 1985.

Influences On The Funds Rate

The funds rate generally reflects the availability of bank reserves. For example, if the Fed should move to increase the supply of bank reserves relative to the demand for reserves, the funds rate should move lower. Conversely, Fed efforts to tighten the supply of reserves relative to bank demands should exert upward pressure on the funds rate.

However, special factors can influence the funds rate independently from reserve availability. In mid-1984 in the wake of the Continental Illinois Bank crisis, banks suddenly turned away from the Fed discount window and fell back heavily on the funds market (dependence on the discount window being viewed as a symptom of financial weakness in view of Continental's heavy dependence on it). This sudden surge in bank demand for funds pushed the funds rate temporarily about one percentage point higher than it otherwise might have been based on reserve availability.

In addition, the funds rate can be influenced by the *distribution* of reserves within the banking system. For example, early in each month there are heavy government outpayments for social security, railroad retirement, and defense which tend to shift funds away from money center banks (the usual borrowers of funds) in favor of smaller banks (the usual lenders of funds). This maldistribution of reserves tends to cause the money center banks to bid more aggressively for funds, thus causing an early-month increase in the level of the funds rate, for any given amount of overall reserve availability in the banking system. In contrast, heavier tax receipts later in each month tend to result in a reverse shift in reserve distribution in favor of the money center banks, thus causing them to bid less aggressively for funds and thereby exerting downward pressure on the funds rate later in the month.

A special case of the maldistribution of reserves occurred in September and October of 1985 when, for an unprecedented length of time, the Senate delayed an increase in the legal ceiling on the public's holdings of Treasury debt. As a result, there was a major interruption in the schedule of new Treasury debt offerings. As the Treasury was forced to reduce its cash balance to unusually low levels to finance its routine outpayments, the money center banks (which are usually the beneficiaries of the bulk of the Treasury's tax and loan balances, as well as of the proceeds of new Treasury debt offerings) tended to lose reserves to the smaller banks. This special maldistribution of reserves caused money center banks to bid more aggressively for funds than otherwise would have been the case, and thus exerted upward pressure on the funds rate.

Psychology

Still another special influence on the funds rate is market psychology. For instance, if funds market participants are expecting a Fed move to tighten reserve pressures, bidders for funds step up to borrow before the expected Fed tightening move occurs; sellers of funds try to hold back and post higher rates in anticipation of the same event. This firming psychology can push the funds rate as much as one-quarter to one-half of a percentage point higher than would otherwise be the case based on reserve availability. Conversely, a dose of easing-funds-market psychology can have the same effect, but in the opposite direction.

The Funds Rate As A Forecasting Tool

Fed watchers may find the federal funds rate the perfect anchor, or starting point, for projecting other interest rates. In such a forecast, the funds rate will be the rate most immediately influenced by Fed policy shifts. (Fed policy shifts, in turn, are influenced by real GNP growth and monetary growth.) Once the funds rate has been projected, the prime rate can be forecast, based on the funds rate as the primary cost of overnight bank funds together with an allowance for credit demands and loan default risks. Taking into account inflationary expectations, the Fed watcher can then project longer-term interest rates such as the 30-year Treasury bond rate and mortgage rates.

To illustrate how this process works, it is possible to make a forecast of interest rates for the four quarters in a future hypothetical year. To set the stage for this hypothetical year's forecast, let's assume that in the preceding year the monetary authorities maintained an accommodative stance. At the same time Federal borrowing demands continued excessively high owing to an out-of-control Federal deficit. Also consumer and business debt expansion continued very strong. Moreover, let's assume that the Fed continued to ease reserve pressures, despite a surge in money growth, mostly because of the need to support a coordinated international effort to push a strong dollar lower and to stimulate growth to help solve debt problems.

In the first half of the future hypothetical year, interest rates are likely to move lower. Behind this decline in interest rates will be sluggish economic activity—reflecting weakness in the manufacturing, energy, and agricultural sectors. Also exerting downward pressure on interest rates will be an accommodative monetary policy, highlighted by two Fed moves to cut the discount rate in the first half of the hypothetical year. Inflationary pressures will be lessened in the first half of the hypothetical year by a plunge in oil prices.

In the second half of the hypothetical year, contrasting upward pressures will be exerted on interest rates as economic activity is given a boost by improving consumer purchasing power (reflecting declining oil prices) and by a declining dollar that results in expanding exports and a declining trade deficit. Also exerting upward pressure on interest rates will be declining inflow of foreign savings to help finance the still large U.S. budget deficit. Inflationary pressures will increase in the second half of the hypothetical year, reflecting the weaker dollar. Belated Fed move to tighten reserve pressures may also add to the upward pressures on interest rates in the second half of the hypothetical year.

TABLE 9-2
Interest rate forecast

	Hypothetical Future Year			
	I	*II*	*III*	*IV*
Federal funds rate	7	6-1/2	7-1/2	8-1/2
Prime rate	9	8-1/2	9-1/2	10-1/2
30-year Treasury rate	7-1/2	7	8	9
Mortgage rates	9-1/2	9	10	11
Real GNP	3.0	2.0	4.0	5.0
GNP deflator	2.5	1.0	2.5	4.5

These forecasts anticipate that the growth in money velocity (GNP/M-1) will continue to decline in the first half of the hypothetical year, after falling in the preceding year. However, in the second half of the hypothetical year, growth in money velocity may turn modestly higher (perhaps rising at a 1–2% annual rate compared to the normal historical average gain of 2–3%). This would occur as the public reduces money balance growth in relation to economic activity (GNP) growth, because of the attraction of rising interest rates on alternative money market investments.

Chapter 10

Federal Reserve Policy, Government Borrowing Demands, and Real Interest Rates[1]

Largely reflecting the interaction among excessive federal borrowing demands, contrasting monetary restraint, and a related sharp decline in inflationary expectations, real interest rates (nominal rates less inflationary expectations)[2] remained at near-record levels over the period from 1981 to 1985 (see Chart 10–1). The persistence of high real interest rates, in turn, threatened to trigger a financial crisis.

To be sure, the Reagan Administration's huge deficits—stemming from large multi-year tax cuts and increased spending (particularly in the defense area)—operated to provide considerable "Keynesian type" fiscal stimulus for the economy in 1983 and 1984. Nevertheless, continuing high real interest rates gave the expansion a unique "built-in" vulnerability. Specifically, debt-heavy borrowers (foreign and domestic) found it increasingly difficult to repay their debts. For many banks, this meant bad loans, poor profits, and deteriorating capital positions.

CHART 10-1
Commercial paper rate and inflationary expectations

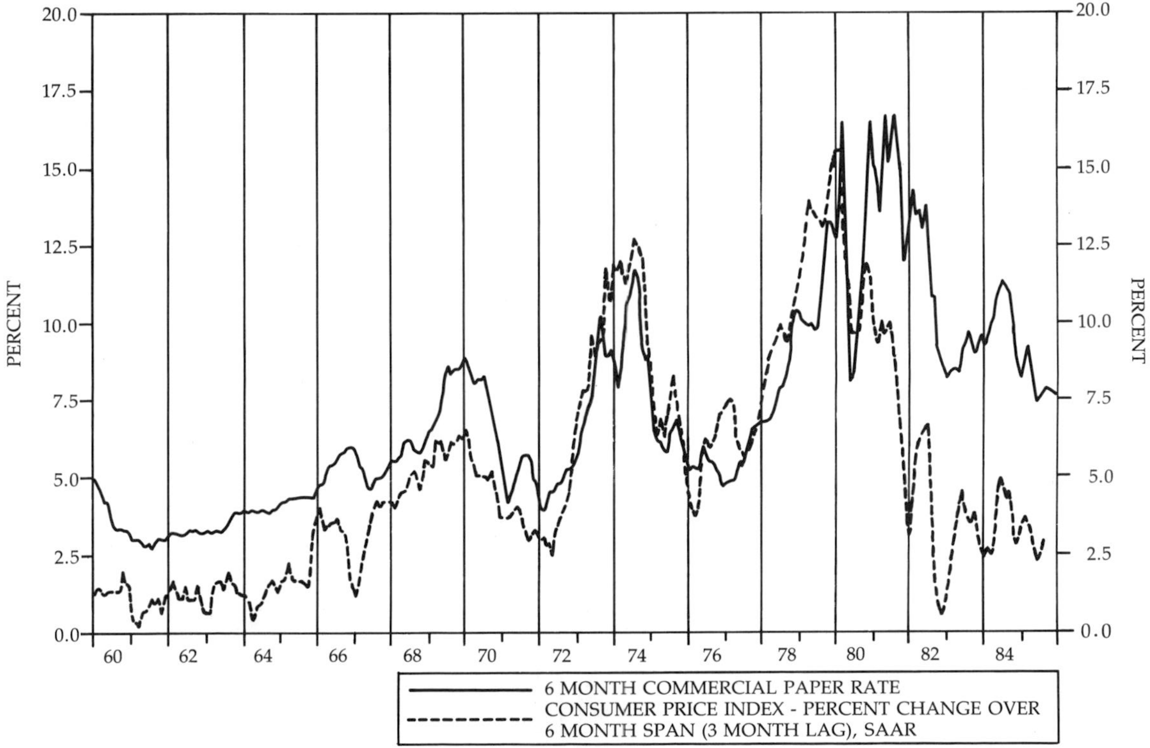

6 MONTH COMMERCIAL PAPER RATE
CONSUMER PRICE INDEX - PERCENT CHANGE OVER
6 MONTH SPAN (3 MONTH LAG), SAAR

PERCENT

114

"Liquidity scares" of the type triggered in the wake of the 1984 Continental Illinois Bank crisis caused nervous large depositors to shift funds from weak to strong banks and from banks into "safer" money market instruments such as Treasury bills.

At the same time, many banks tightened credit standards, and reduced farm and foreign lending to try to rebuild capital adequacy. For a number of banks these efforts resulted in a reduction of total asset and liability footings and such actions inevitably tended to depress economic growth and to contribute to deflationary pressures.

Precarious Policy Mismatch

More by accident than by the design of Reagan economic policy, the 1983–1985 economic expansion was characterized by the favorable forces of brisk real growth (at least in the first two years of this period) and unexpectedly low inflation. At the same time, about 10 million new non-farm payroll jobs were created in this impressive economic expansion. Actually, this expansion has been founded on what might be called a "precarious policy mismatch." The causal chain started with the Reagan Administration's largely unintended mismatch between strong fiscal stimulus and moderate monetary restraint (at least through 1984).

The Reagan Administration certainly intended a smaller and less stimulative federal deficit by the third year of expansion. Specifically, President Reagan's simple fiscal policy approach was aimed at getting the federal government "off the backs" of middle and upper income taxpayers (his main constituents).[3] To accomplish this, President Reagan sought huge tax cuts, apparently aimed at "capping" federal revenue at 20% or less of GNP. In addition, the President hoped to force Congress to cut nondefense spending sufficiently to balance the budget no later than 1984.

The only problem was that President Reagan concurrently sought to sharply increase defense spending in order to beef up U.S. military strength. At the same time, Federal spending on social security and other mostly middle-income entitlement programs soared. Thus, while President Reagan was able, by fiscal 1985, to successfully push Federal revenues to below 19% of GNP, he lost control on the spending side. Specifically, federal spending, as a percent of GNP was climbing sharply higher to about 24% in 1985. The unintended result was that, contrary to the pattern of sharp deficit declines in previous cyclical periods of strong expansion, the federal deficit (including off-budget borrowing) remained high at $185 billion in fiscal year 1984 and climbed even higher to $212 billion in fiscal 1985.

What made the Reagan Administration's fiscal stimulus unique, however, was that it was accompanied—following an initial dose of aggressive Federal Reserve accommodation in the second half of 1982 and early 1983—by moderate monetary restraint (more or less sanctioned by the Reagan Administration). This Fed restraint was reflected in markedly slower M-1 growth in the second half of 1983 and in 1984. For example, after M-1 growth had surged at an expansionary pace of more than 12% in both the last half of 1982 and the first half of 1983, it then dropped sharply to a more restrictive 5.5% annual rate of increase in the last half of 1983. In 1984, M-1 growth dropped still lower to a pace of about 5%, which rested in the lower half of the Fed's 4–8% M-1 target range for 1984.

Federal Borrowing Pressures and Strains on Savings Flows

Conceptually, it is appropriate to view *nominal* interest rates as determined by the interaction between total government and private credit *demands* (plus the nonbank public's demands for money balances) in relation to the *supply* of savings (plus new money growth).[4] To derive *real*, or inflation-adjusted, interest rates, it is necessary to subtract inflationary expectations from nominal interest rates. As envisioned by lenders and borrowers, these inflationary expectations are founded on either current inflation or some distributed lag of past inflation.

Actually, Federal Reserve efforts to ease (tighten) bank reserve pressures in order to increase (decrease) money growth can impact *real* interest rates in two ways. Typically, Fed actions to ease (tighten) reserve pressures and to increase (decrease) money growth initially cause nominal (and real) interest rates to decline (increase). But, in the special case, when inflation expectations increase because sustained or aggressive Fed easing actions are *perceived* by borrowers and lenders as being excessive and potentially inflationary, *real* interest rates may temporarily decline more sharply than nominal rates. Such a development was particularly evident in the period from late 1974 through 1976. Of course, increased inflationary expectations may eventually stimulate increased private borrowing demands or reduced savings, thereby increasing nominal interest rates.

Conversely, when Fed tightening moves are perceived as excessive and potentially deflationary, real interest rates may increase more sharply than nominal rates. In the last half of 1983 and again in the last six months of 1984, there were apparent major downward adjustments in lender and borrower inflationary expectations. These downward adjustments in inflationary expectations seem to have partly reflected Fed restrictive moves in the first half of each of these years. Thus, in such circumstances, real interest rates are likely to remain abnormally high and may potentially depress private borrowing and spending.

As can be seen in Chart 10–2, from 1970 through 1974, the federal borrowings component of total credit demands was relatively stable. During this period, total federal debt (including federal agency debt) remained comfortably sta-

CHART 10-2
Debt of domestic nonfinancial sectors (seasonally adjusted)

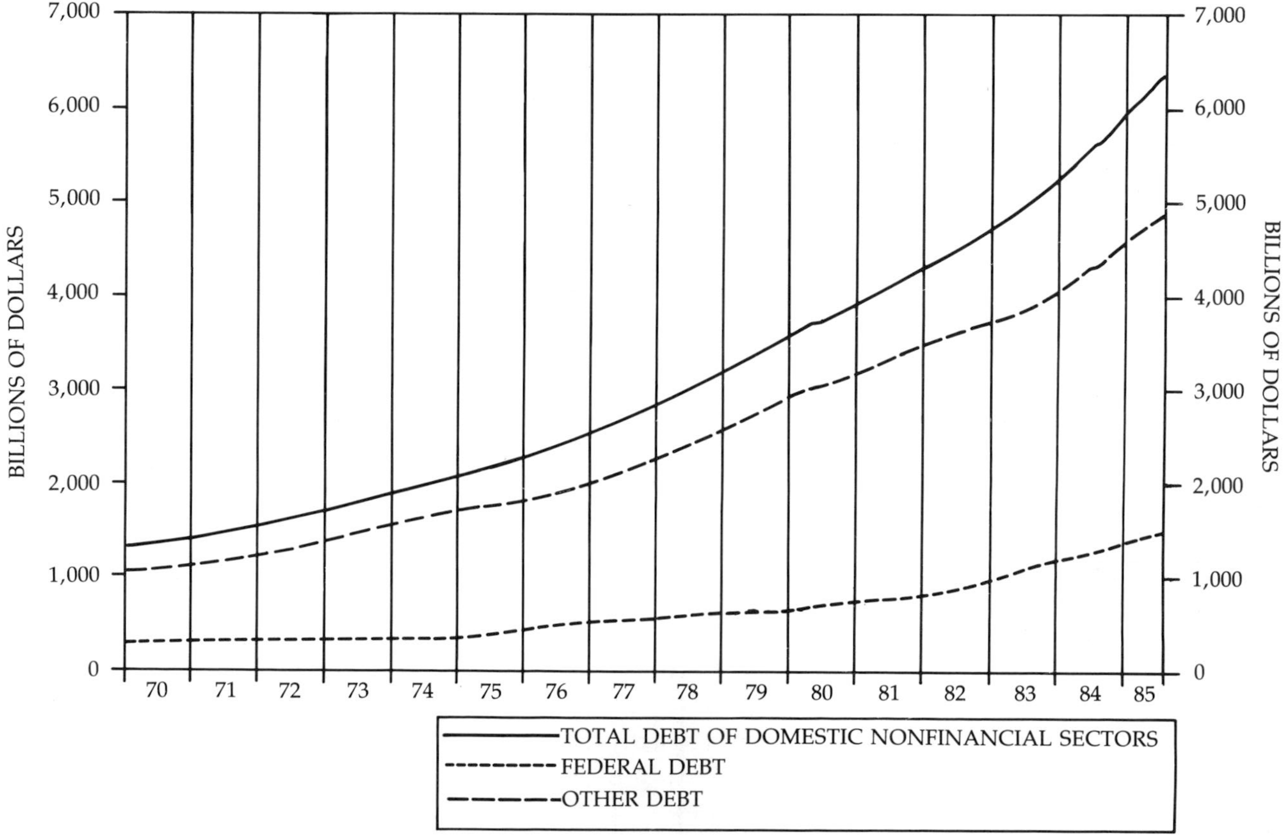

BILLIONS OF DOLLARS

TOTAL DEBT OF DOMESTIC NONFINANCIAL SECTORS
- - - - FEDERAL DEBT
- — - OTHER DEBT

ble under $500 billion. But a contrasting rapid climb in federal debt began in 1975, and steepened ominously at the beginning of 1982. The increasingly rapid ascent lifted the federal debt total to nearly $2 trillion by the end of 1985.

The ratio of federal debt to total domestic nonfinancial debt (including consumer, mortgage, municipal, and business debt) actually declined from just under 22% at the beginning of 1970 to just over 17% by the end of 1974, as can be seen in Chart 10–3. By contrast, during the 1974–76 period of recession and early recovery, the ratio of federal debt to domestic nonfinancial debt increased to just under 21%. Then, by early 1980, in the face of surging inflationary speculation and private debt expansion, this ratio eased back to just over 18%. By the end of 1985, this federal debt–total debt ratio had made a countercyclical upward move toward 24%. However, at least a whiff of fiscal restraint was in the air as 1985 came to a close. The late-1985 Gramm-Rudman law, perhaps the most bizarre piece of legislation ever passed, seeks to balance the federal budget by 1991. Should the President and Congress be unable to agree on the required annual deficit-cutting steps, the Gramm-Rudman process provided for automatic across-the-board spending cuts (with some exceptions) to achieve the budget-balancing objective. The precise size of the deficit and therefore of the "automatic" cuts was to be determined by the General Accounting Office (GAO), based on the information from the Congressional Budget Office (CBO) and Office of Management and the Budget (OMB). However, this automatic deficit-cutting feature was declared unconstitutional by the Supreme Court. In anticipation of this possibility, the Gramm-Rudman measure provided for a fall back solution. Specifically, Congress is to incorporate the deficit-cutting measures necessary to balance the budget by 1991 into annual joint resolutions which must be passed by Congress and sent to the President for his signature.

A convenient if simplistic measure of the degree of pressure that federal government borrowing demands are

CHART 10-3
Ratio of federal debt to total debt of domestic nonfinancial sectors (S.A.)
(monthly 1970–1985)

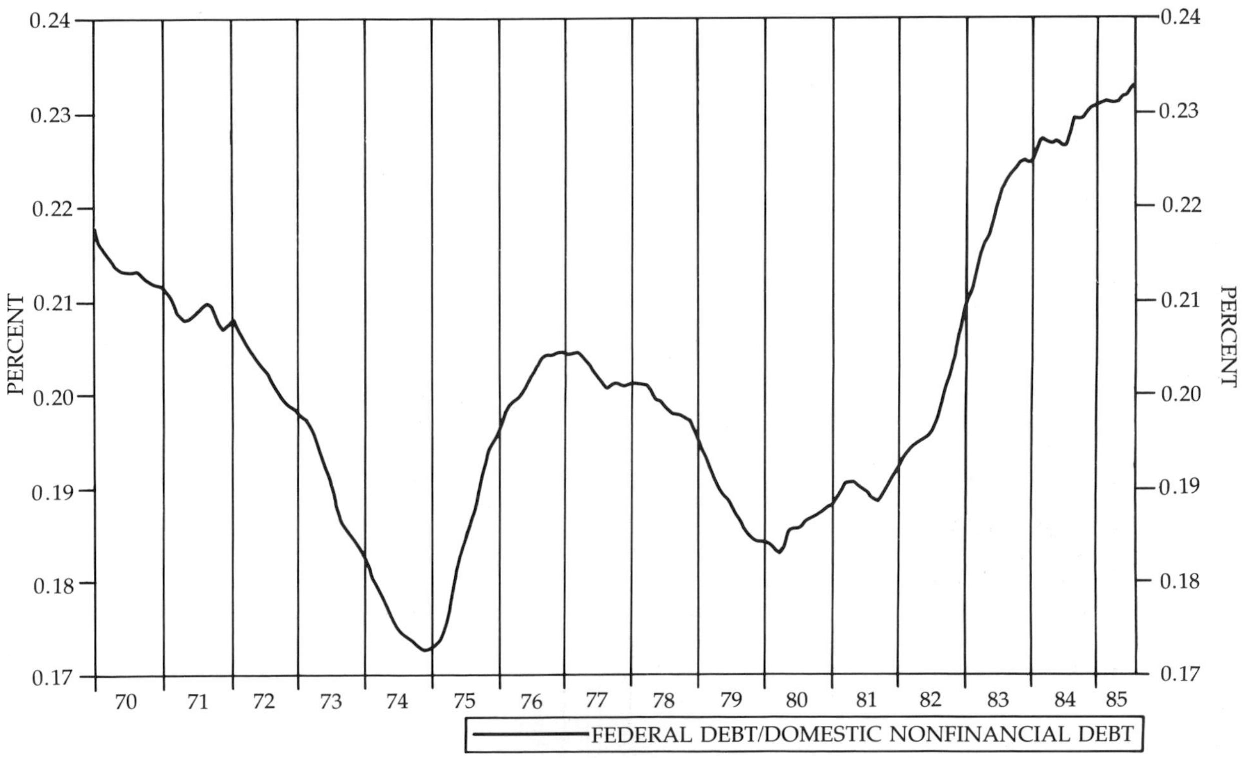

FEDERAL DEBT/DOMESTIC NONFINANCIAL DEBT

CHART 10-4

Government borrowing as a percentage of domestic savings (quarterly 1960–1985)

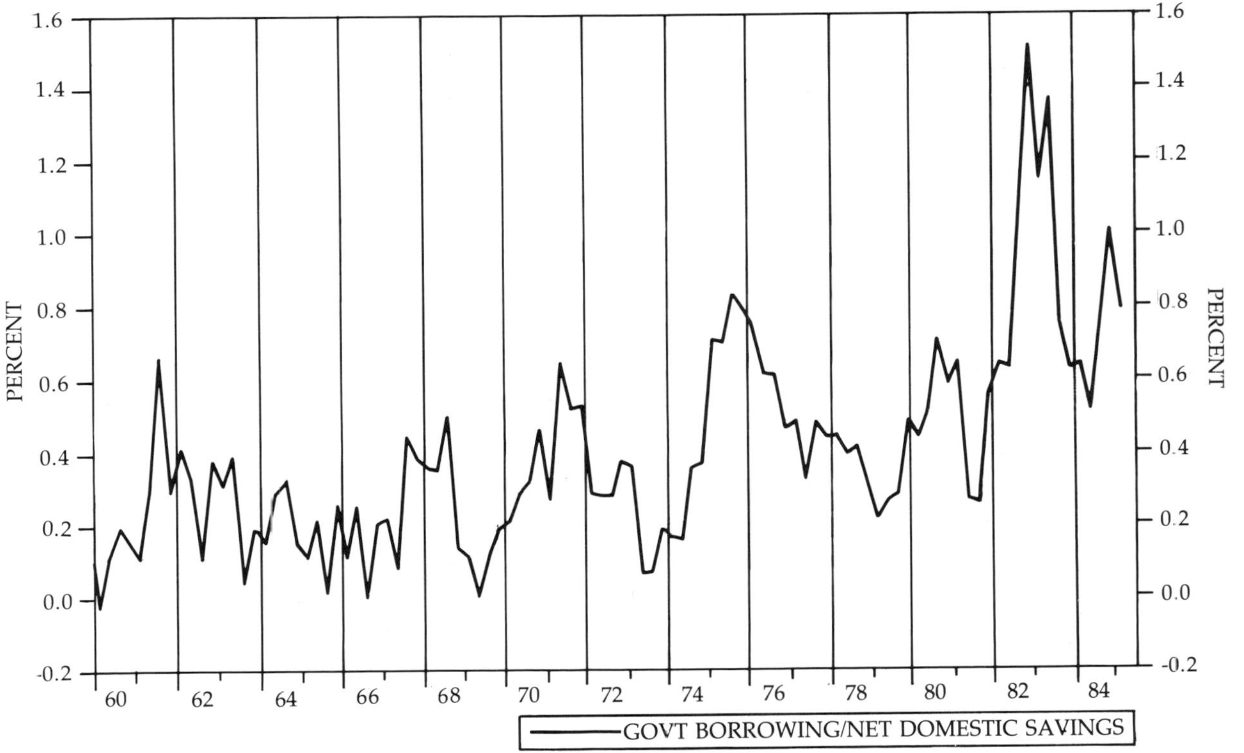

GOVT BORROWING/NET DOMESTIC SAVINGS

exerting on the supply of savings—and thus on nominal interest rates—is the ratio of government borrowings to (net) domestic savings (see Chart 10–4). During the 1960s, this ratio averaged 22%, but subsequently nearly doubled to an average of 40% during the 1970s. However, this step-up in government borrowing pressure did not translate into upward pressure on real interest rates, due to sharply rising lender and borrower inflationary expectations during this decade.

This finding is significant. It suggests that high real interest rates must always be viewed as the product not only of excessive government borrowing but of factors that influence inflationary expectations. Among the influences on inflationary expectations could be exogenous factors such as oil and food shortages, or even Fed anti-inflation credibility. Of course, endogenous factors such as the rate of industrial capacity utilization, the unemployment rate, wage rates, and productivity growth also influence both inflation and inflationary expectations.

During the period from 1980 to 1985, the average ratio of government borrowings to (net) domestic savings soared to heretofore unimagined heights of 72%. More significantly, in sharp contrast to the 1970s, additional upward pressure was exerted on real interest rates, due to a significant decline in inflationary expectations during 1983 and 1984. This dampening of inflationary prospects was aided by a surge in Fed anti-inflation credibility.

Net Foreign Investment

Undoubtedly, the upward pressure on real interest rates stemming from increasing government borrowing demands and declining inflationary expectations during the current expansion would have been substantially greater had it not been for a sharp increase in net foreign investment in the U.S. during the period from 1983 through

CHART 10-5

Net foreign investment (quarterly 1960–1985)
(billions of dollars)

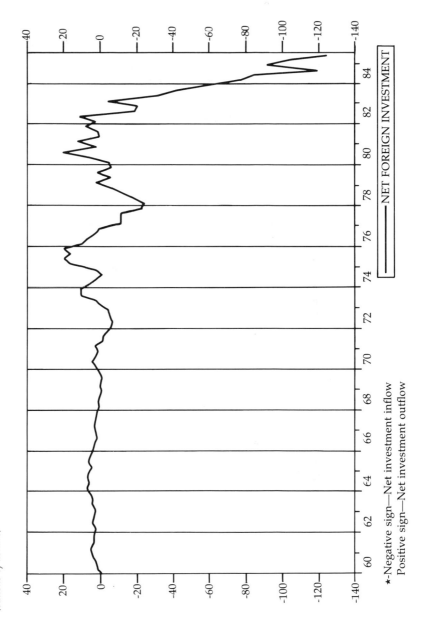

★–Negative sign—Net investment inflow
Positive sign—Net investment outflow

——— NET FOREIGN INVESTMENT

1985. By the final quarter of 1985, net foreign investment soared to an annual rate approaching $140 billion (see Chart 10–5). This foreign investment is, of course, the direct counterpart of a deepening U.S. trade deficit.

In essence, this inflow of foreign funds can be viewed as an addition to (net) domestic savings available to meet government and private credit demands. At the same time, it is important to note that these net inflows of funds are not determined solely by decisions of foreigners to invest in the U.S. Net foreign investment has also been influenced by a sharp reduction in foreign lending by U.S. banks. A shift by U.S. corporations in favor of overseas borrowing and a decline in foreign borrowing in U.S. financial markets has also impacted the net foreign investment total.

Looking ahead, however, this inflow of foreign investment is likely to diminish in accordance with a declining U.S. dollar and an expected contraction in the U.S. trade deficit. As a result, the only avenue to lower real rates is a significant reduction in the federal budget deficit, or a major surge in domestic savings (which seems unlikely). Of course, the alternative of excessive monetary ease is available. This would reignite inflationary expectations, and drive real rates lower for a time; but clearly this policy approach is unacceptable.

Chapter 11

Conclusions

The secret to successful investing in the bond and stock markets has been unlocked. Be a Fed watcher! Get to know the thinking of the Fed Chairman and other key Fed policy makers. Assemble a tool kit of certain items to watch more closely than others and be sure that these are the same items that Fed policy makers watch most closely. The most helpful "tool kit" components are quarterly real GNP growth, monthly M-1 growth, and bank borrowings at the Fed discount window. One advantage of having more than one item in the Fed watching "tool kit" is that this approach is useful despite changes in basic Fed policy emphasis over the business cycle.

Currently, the "art" of central banking seems to be evolving into an asymmetrical approach. In cyclical phases when combating inflation is the main objective, Fed policy makers focus on effectively disciplining monetary growth. But, contrastingly, during periods when the Fed's policy focus shifts to the need to stimulate sluggish economic activity, the main object of its attention becomes real GNP growth. In this case, Fed responses to excessive M-1 growth may be delayed for some time.

Of course, under special circumstances, the Fed may delay moves to tighten reserve pressures in response to excessive increases in either real GNP or money growth. This might occur during periods of special financial tensions or undesired dollar strength. In such a situation, the best "tool kit" item to follow would be bank borrowings at the Fed discount window. A stable borrowings level means that the Fed is intending to maintain unchanged pressures on bank reserves and thus is continuing to delay its response to undesired money or real GNP movements.

Using this Fed watching "tool kit" investors can anticipate most Fed policy shifts. These Fed policy shifts are a major influence on the federal funds rate and other money market rates.

The most important point for Fed watchers to remember is that there is no magic formula for monetary policy. No flawless process exists whereby Fed policy makers can set a "dial" for bank reserve pressures to once and for all result in a "perfect" rate of money and credit growth and, in turn, a "perfect" maximum rate of noninflationary economic growth.

Quite the contrary. Monetary policy has evolved as a subjective process; it should be viewed as an art, not a science. The policy process is based on continuous Fed readings of incoming economic and monetary data; the Fed officials respond to these readings with frequent adjustments in bank reserve pressures.

In this effort the monetary authorities focus most of their attention not on total reserves but on the nonborrowed and borrowed reserve components of the reserve total. Thus, when Fed officials perceive that the economy is growing at an excessive and potentially inflationary pace, they seek to tighten bank reserve pressures by making it more difficult and costly for banks to obtain *nonbor-*

rowed reserves. This forces banks to temporarily fall back on the discount window for extra *borrowed* reserves as a stop-gap measure. In this instance, the Fed increases its operating target accordingly for such *borrowed* reserves.

However, as banks scramble to extricate themselves from the Fed discount window, they can be expected to bid up the rates on federal funds, RPs, CDs, Eurodollars, and other sources of lendable funds. Higher interest rates on bank lendable funds are, in turn, passed on as an increase in the prime rate and other rates charged business and consumer borrowers. Eventually, consumers and businesses may find their increased borrowing costs prohibitive—certainly this was the case in the early 1980s. The result is a slowing of economic activity and the rate of money and credit growth to a less inflationary pace.

Regardless of how haphazard the contemporary development of this monetary policy process, and how imperfect and subjective it may be, the fact is that it has worked when it has been most needed. Indeed, the tortuous evolution of modern central banking techniques reached a pinnacle of sorts during the early 1980s when the Fed helped crush the forces of inflation and inflationary expectations through its efforts to establish monetary discipline.

As a general rule, a Fed tightening in reserve pressures (as reflected in an increase in the federal funds rate and other market rates) should promptly begin to exert upward pressure on bond yields and have a depressing influence on stock prices soon thereafter. A sustained increase in interest rates hurts the stock market in two ways: Higher interest rates make bonds more attractive investments than stocks, and rising interest rates eventually weaken economic activity and depress the profits outlook. Conversely, under most circumstances, a Fed easing in reserve pressures and a related decline in the funds rate will exert downward pressure on bond yields and in turn, sparks an increase in stock prices on the heels of the improving bond market.

   This system is simple, but it may help investors make more sense of bond yield and stock market movements.

Chapter Notes

Introduction—The Basics

1. More specifically, the stated purpose of the original *Federal Reserve Act* of December 23, 1913 was "To provide for the establishment of Federal reserve banks, to furnish an elastic currency, to afford means of discounting commercial paper, to establish a more effective supervision of banking in the United States, and for other purposes." Furthermore, as amended on October 27, 1978, the *Federal Reserve Act* states, under section (2A), that "The Board of Governors of the Federal Reserve and the Federal Open Market Committee shall maintain long run growth of the monetary and credit aggregates commensurate with the economy's long run potential to increase production, so as to promote effectively the goals of maximum employment, stable prices, and moderate long-term interest rates."

2. *Ibid.*, pp. 3, 20.

Chapter 1

1. Lester V. Chandler, *Benjamin Strong, Central Banker*, (Washington D.C.: The Brookings Institution, 1958), p. 1.

2. Stephen V.O. Clarke, *Central Bank Cooperation 1924–1931*, (New York: Federal Reserve Bank of New York, 1967), pp. 88–89.

3. See: Federal Reserve. Board of Governors, *Tenth Annual Report for 1923*, p. 13; and Chandler, *Benjamin Strong, Central Banker*, p. 209.

4. *Ibid.*, pp. 199–204.

5. Marriner S. Eccles, "The Lessons of Monetary Experience," *Essays in Honor of Irving Fisher* (New York: Farrar and Rinehart, 1937).

6. *Ibid.*

7. *Ibid.*, p. 13.

8. *Ibid.*, p. 4.

9. *Ibid.*, p. 16.

10. Sidney Hyman, *Marriner S. Eccles: Private Entrepreneur and Public Servant,* (Stanford, California: Stanford University Graduate School of Business, 1976), p. 350.

11. *Ibid.*, pp. 343–351.

12. William McChesney Martin, Jr., Statement in Richard E. Mooney and Edwin L. Dale, Jr., eds., *Inflation and Recession*, (New York: Doubleday & Co. Inc., 1958), p. 23.

13. *Ibid.*, p. 16.

14. *Ibid.*, p. 17.

15. Federal Reserve. Board of Governors, *Annual Report for 1968*, pp. 167–174.

16. Cary Reich, "Inside the Fed," *Institutional Investor Magazine*, (May, 1984), p. 139.

17. *Ibid.*, p. 139.

18. Paul A. Volcker, *Statement before the U.S. Congress, Joint Economic Committee*, (June 15, 1982), p. 2.

19. For a discussion of the empirical evidence on the relative effects of these alternate approaches to controlling money, see: Stephen H. Axilrod and David E. Lindsey, "Federal Reserve Implementation of Monetary Policy: Analytical Foundations of the New Approach," *American Economic Review, Papers and Proceedings*, (May, 1981), pp. 246–252.

Chapter 2

1. As examples of contemporary literature that are available on the impact of weekly money supply movements on the financial markets, see, for example:

Kurt Dew, "Practical Monetarism and the Stock Market," Federal Reserve Bank of San Francisco, *Economic Review*, (Spring, 1978).

Neil G. Berkman, "On the Significance of Weekly Changes in M-1," Federal Reserve Bank of Boston, *New England Economic Report*, (May/June, 1978).

William T. Garvin and Nicholas V. Karamouzis, "The Reserve Market and the Information Content of M-1 Announcements," Federal Reserve Bank of Cleveland, *Economic Review*, (IQ: 1985).

Richard G. Sheehan, "Weekly Money Announcements: New Information and Its Effects," Federal Reserve Bank of St. Louis, *Review*, August/September, 1985.

Chapter 3

1. For an excellent analysis of the economic policy implications of the Employment Act of 1946, see: Arthur F. Burns, *The Business Cycle in a Changing World*, (New York: National Bureau of Economic Research, 1969), pp. 221–231.

2. Federal Reserve. Board of Governors, *Annual Report for 1978*, pp. 338–340.

3. For an up-to-date description of the Federal Reserve's Capacity Utilization series, see: Richard D. Raddock, "Revised Federal Reserve Rates of Capacity Utilization," Federal Reserve Board of Governors, *Federal Reserve Bulletin*, (October, 1985), pp. 754–766.

Chapter 4

1. For an excellent discussion of the role of monetary aggregates as intermediate Fed targets, see: Stephen H. Axilrod, "Monetary Policy, Money Supply, and the Federal Reserve's Operating Proceedings," Federal Reserve Board of Governors, Federal Reserve *Bulletin*, (January, 1982), pp. 13–24.

2. The M-2 aggregate is defined as M-1 plus savings and small time deposits (issued in amounts of less than $100,000) plus money market demand accounts plus money market fund balances (general purpose and broker-dealer) plus overnight RPs and overnight Eurodollars. The still broader M-3 aggregate is defined as M-2 plus large time deposits (issued in amounts of $100,000 or more) plus money market fund balances (institutional) plus term RPs and term Eurodollars.

3. For a discussion of credit aggregates, see: Richard G. Davis, "Board Credit Measures as Targets for Monetary Policy," Federal Reserve Bank of New York, *Quarterly Review*, Summer, 1979; Benjamin M. Friedman, "The Relative Stability of Money and Credit Velocities in the United States: Evidence and Some Speculations," *Working Paper No. 645*, (National Bureau of Economic Research, 1981); and Benjamin M. Friedman, "Monetary Policy with a Credit

Aggregate Target," in Karl Brunner and Allan H. Meltzer, eds. *Money, Monetary Policy, and Financial Institutions*, Carnegie-Rochester Conference Series on Public Policy (Spring 1983), and Edward K. Offenbacher and Richard D. Porter, "Empirical Comparisons of Credit and Monetary Aggregate, Using Vector Autoregression Methods," Special Studies Paper 181, Federal Reserve Board of Governors (October 1983).

4. For a thorough analysis of postwar trends in money velocity over the period from 1947 to 1960, see: Milton Friedman and Anna J. Schwartz, *A Monetary History of the United States 1867–1960*, (Princeton, N.J.: Princeton University Press, 1963) pp. 639–675. See also: George Garvy and Martin R. Blyn, *The Velocity of Money*, Federal Reserve Bank of New York, 1969, pp. 78–94.

5. See: Michael J. Hamburger, "Money Growth Is Not Excessive," *Economic Insights*, Michael J. Hamburger and Associates, Inc. in association with Keane Securities, (August, 1985).

6. For a discussion of the impact of "stable" or improving economic conditions on money velocity, see: Friedman, *A Monetary History of the United States 1867–1960*, pp. 673–675.

7. An analysis of this type of decline in money velocity can be found in: John P. Judd, "The Recent Decline in Velocity: Instability in Money Demand or Inflation?" Federal Reserve Bank of San Francisco, *Economic Review*, (Spring, 1983), pp. 12–19.

8. For a general discussion of the problems of measuring velocity in a period of a sharply increasing trade deficit, see: Lawrence J. Radecki and John Wenninger, "Recent Instability in M-1's Velocity," Federal Reserve Bank of New York, *Quarterly Review*, (Autumn, 1985), pp. 16–22.

9. *Debits to Demand Deposits* (Quarter-to-Quarter percentage change at an annual rate—measured from last month of quarter)

	1985			
	I	II	III	IV
All Insured Banks	6.1	20.4	35.1	74.2
Major NYC Banks	1.2	26.2	36.9	91.5
Other Banks	10.2	15.6	33.6	59.7

10. Stephen H. Axilrod, "Discussion," Proceedings of a Conference Held at Melvin Village, New Hampshire, *Controlling Monetary Aggregates III*, Federal Reserve Bank of Boston, (October, 1980), p. 306.

11. Goldfeld estimated a conventional money demand equation:

$$MD_t = a + bY - cr_t - dr_c + eM_{t-1}$$

where: MD is the public's demand for money in period (t); Y is gross national product; r_t is the interest rate on time deposits; and r_c is the interest rate on commercial paper.

Goldfeld estimated this equation quarterly for a sample period from 1952 II to 1973 IV. The equation was then dynamically simulated for the ten-quarter, out-of-sample period beginning in 1974 I and ending in 1976 II. See: Stephen M. Goldfeld, "The Case of the Missing Money," *Brookings Papers on Economic Activity, 3: 1976,* (Washington, D.C.: The Brookings Institution).

12. See: Jared Enzler, Lewis Johnson, and John Paulus, "Some Problems of Money Demand," *Brookings Papers on Economic Activity, 1: 1976,* (Washington, D.C.: The Brookings Institution).

13. For an analysis of the *underpredicting* tendencies of money demand estimates, see: John Wenninger, "The M-1–GNP Relationship: A Component Approach," Federal Reserve Bank of New York, *Quarterly Review,* (Autumn, 1984), pp. 6–15.

Chapter 5

1. The conventional statement of the reserve-deposit multiplier is:

$$D^* = R \cdot \frac{1}{r} = \frac{R}{r}$$

where D^* is the maximum deposit level the banking system can support; R is total reserves; r is the legal ratio of required reserves to deposits. Thus, if R is 5, and r is .10, then D^* is 50. For the earliest clear exposition of the deposit expansion multiplier, see: C.A. Phillips, *Bank Credit,* (New York: Macmillan Company, 1920), pp. 32–76.

2. See: Richard L. Mugel, "Reserve Borrowings and the Money Market," Federal Reserve Bank of Cleveland, *Economic Commentary,* (November 11, 1985).

3. Robert V. Roosa, "Credit Policy at the Discount Window: Comment," *Quarterly Journal of Economics,* (May, 1959), p. 334.

4. Federal Reserve, Board of Governors, and the United States Treasury, *The Federal Reserve and the Treasury: Answers to Questions from the Commission on Money and Credit,* (Englewood Cliffs, N.J.: Prentice-Hall, Inc., 1963), p. 118.

Chapter 6

1. Federal Reserve Board of Governors, Annual Report for 1966, pp, 147–148.

2. It should be noted that, in the period from February 1972 to March 1976, Fed efforts to control money growth from the demand side through modest adjustments in the federal funds rate were complemented by a more direct reserve control approach. Specifically, the Fed introduced a new reserve target—reserves available to support private nonbank deposits (RPDs). At each FOMC meeting the Fed set a new two-month target range for RPD growth. The

main problem with this generally unsuccessful experiment was that the Fed nearly always missed its target for RPD growth. Moreover, the Fed was frequently making major adjustments in its target range for two-month RPD growth.

3. Henry C. Wallich, "Changes in Monetary Policy and the Fight Against Inflation," Remarks to the Cato Institute, January 21, 1983, p. 2.

4. Federal Reserve Board of Governors, "Record of the Federal Open Market Committee, October 6, 1979," *Federal Reserve Bulletin* (December, 1979), p. 974.

5. Henry C. Wallich, "Recent Techniques of Monetary Policy," Remarks to the Midwest Finance Association, April 5, 1984, pp. 11–12.

Chapter 7

1. See: Blanca Riemer, "The 'Gang of Four' is Ganging Up on Volcker," *Business Week Magazine*, December 23, 1985, pp. 60–61.

2. See: Rowland Evans and Robert Novak, "Backstage at the Fed," *Washington Post*, (March 17, 1986; Paul Blustein and Allan Murray, "Vote on Discount Rate Cut Was A Defeat for Volcker By Reagan Appointees," *Wall Street Journal*, (March 18, 1986); and John M. Berry, "Board Discount Rate Cut Followed Tortuous Trail," *Washington Post*, (March 19, 1986).

Chapter 8

1. The term "real bills" was coined in: L.W. Mints, *A History of Banking Theory in Great Britain and the United States*, (Chicago: University of Chicago Press, 1945), p. 9.

2. See: Federal Reserve. Board of Governors, *Tenth Annual Report for 1923*, p. 35.

3. Winfield W. Riefler, *Money Rates and Money Markets in the United States*, (New York: Harper & Brothers, 1930), pp. 18–36.

4. See: Peter D. Sternlight, "Monetary Policy and Open Market Operations in 1984," Federal Reserve Bank of New York, *Quarterly Review*, (Spring, 1985), pp. 36–56.

Chapter 9

1. Perhaps the best studies of the nature and early evolution of the federal funds market are: Federal Reserve. Board of Governors, *The Federal Funds Market—A Study by a Federal Reserve System Committee*, (May, 1959); Parker B. Willis, *The Federal Funds Market* (Boston: The Federal Reserve Bank of Boston, 1964); Federal Reserve

Board of Governors, *A Study of the Market for Federal Funds*, prepared in connection with the Federal Reserve System's Reappraisal of the Discount Mechanism, (March 28, 1967); and Dorothy M. Nichols, *Trading in Federal Funds*, (Washington, D.C.: Federal Reserve, Board of Governors, 1965).

2. See: George W. McKinney, Jr. and David M. Jones, "Innovation in American Banking, "*The Banker Magazine*, 119 (January, 1969).

Chapter 10

1. This chapter is largely based on an unpublished paper: David M. Jones, "Treasury Financing and the Impact on the Flow of Funds and Real Interest Rate Levels," presented to the Joint Session on the Outlook for Financial Markets of the American Economic Association and the National Association of Business Economists, Dallas, Texas, December 29, 1984.

2. For the classic discussion of real interest rates, see: Irving Fisher, *The Purchasing Power Of Money*, (New York: Macmillan, 1911).

3. See: Council of Economic Advisers, *Economic Report of the President*, February, 1982, (Washington, D.C.: United States Government Printing Office, 1982), pp. 36–46.

4. See: Joseph W. Conard, *An Introduction to the Theory of Interest Rates*, (Berkeley and Los Angeles: University of California Press, 1959), and *The Behavior of Interest Rates*, (New York: National Bureau of Economic Research, 1966).

*A*ppendixes

*A*_{*ppendix I*}

*D*_{*iscount rate minutes*}

DISCOUNT RATE MINUTES
(Released 11/4/82)

MEETING DATES RELEASED: 1982   10 pages total

July 26	- 1 page
July 29	- 1 page
July 30	- 2 page
August 9	- 1 page
August 13	- 2 page
August 23	- 1 page
August 26	- 2 page

Government in the Sunshine
Supplemental Release of
Information

Board of Governors of the
Federal Reserve System

Meeting date   July 26, 1982, July 29, 1982, July 30, 1982, August 9, 1982,
                       August 13, 1982, August 23, 1982 & August 26, 1982

The following information SUPPLEMENTS the earlier release of recordings and/or minutes for this
meeting.

Release of Recording:

— The recording of the following item(s) is now released in its entirety. (Cassette[s] available for
listening)

Release of Minutes:

X   The minutes for the attached items(s) are now released in their entirety. (See attachment)

Discount Rate Entry

11 - 4 - 82

Date of Release

7/26/82   FOI copy

   <u>Discount rates</u>. In a memorandum dated July 23, 1982, the

Office of the Secretary reported that, subject to review and

determination by the Board of Governors, the directors of the Federal

Reserve Banks of Philadelphia and Chicago had voted on July 22 and the

directors of the Federal Reserve Bank of Atlanta had voted on July 23,

1982, to lower the basic discount rate from its current level of

11-1/2 percent to 11 percent, with corresponding 1/2 percentage point

decreases in related rates. The directors of the Federal Reserve

Banks of Richmond and Dallas had voted to maintain existing rates.

   The Board discussed the appropriateness of lowering the

discount rate and reached agreement that no change in the discount

rate was desirable at this time. Thereupon, the Board <u>deferred</u>

action on the requests. (Participating in this discussion:

Chairman Volcker and Governors Martin, Teeters, and Rice.)

1

7/29/82   FOI copy

Discount Rates.   At its meeting on July 26, 1982, the Board
deferred action on requests by the directors of the Federal Reserve
Banks of Philadelphia, Atlanta, and Chicago to lower the basic
discount rate from its current level of 11-1/2 percent to 11 percent,
with corresponding 1/2 percentage point decreases in related rates.
In a memorandum dated July 29, 1982, the Office of the Secretary
reported that those requests were still pending and that, subject to
review and determination by the Board of Governors, the directors of
the Federal Reserve Bank of Boston had voted on July 28 to establish a
basic rate of 11 percent, with corresponding 1/2 percentage point
decreases in related rates. In addition, the directors of the
Richmond, St. Louis, Kansas City, and Dallas Banks had voted to
maintain existing rates.

The Board's discussion of the requests today disclosed
agreement that a discount rate reduction might be appropriate in the
very near future. It was noted that growth of money and credit had
been restrained in recent weeks and that short-term market rates had
declined on balance. Additional information would become available
tomorrow on key economic indicators and on the monetary aggregates for
the week ending July 14. Although there was a tentative decision to
lower the discount rate today, the Board decided to defer action
pending receipt of that additional information. (Participating in
this discussion: Chairman Volcker and Governors Teeters, Rice, and
Gramley.)

1

7/30/82   FOI copy

Discount rates. At its meeting yesterday, the Board

considered requests from the Federal Reserve Banks of Boston,

Philadelphia, Atlanta, and Chicago to lower the basic discount rate

from 11-1/2 percent to 11 percent, with corresponding 1/2 percentage

point decreases in related rates. In a memorandum dated July 29,

1982, the Office of the Secretary reported that, subject to review

and determination by the Board of Governors, the directors of the

Federal Reserve Banks of New York and San Francisco also had voted

yesterday to establish that reduced schedule of rates. Although a

tentative decision to approve the requests had been expressed at

yesterday's meeting, the Board deferred action pending receipt of

additional economic and monetary data that would be available today.

At today's meeting, the Board noted that the latest economic

data continued to suggest weakness in overall economic activity.

Interest rates had declined appreciably over the course of recent

weeks and the latest data on monetary and credit aggregates continued

to indicate relatively restrained growth. Against this background,

Board members agreed that a 1/2 percentage point reduction in the

schedule of discount rates would be appropriate at this time.

Thereupon, the Board unamimously approved a reduction in the

basic discount rate from 11-1/2 percent to 11 percent, with

corresponding 1/2 percentage point reductions in related rates,

effective August 2, 1982, for the six Banks that had established such

7/30/82   FOI copy

rates. (Voting for this action: Chairman Volcker and Governors
Teeters, Rice, and Gramley.)

The Board authorized issuance of a press release announcing
its action. In addition, the Secretary of the Board was authorized to
inform any other Reserve Bank that established a basic discount rate
of 11 percent, along with appropriate related rates, of the Board's
approval of that schedule of rates.

(Note: Subsequently, advice was received that the directors
of the following Reserve Banks had established the lower rate schedule
and those Banks were informed of the Board's approval, effective the
dates indicated: Richmond, St. Louis, Minneapolis, Kansas City, and
Dallas, effective August 2, 1982, and Cleveland, effective August 3,
1982.)

8/9/82   FOI copy

     <u>Discount rates</u>.   In a memorandum dated August 6, 1982, the Office of
the Secretary reported that, subject to review and determination by the
Board of Governors, the directors of the Federal Reserve Banks of
Philadelphia and Chicago on August 5, and Atlanta on August 6, 1982, had
voted to establish a basic discount rate of 10-1/2 percent (a reduction from
11 percent), with corresponding 1/2 percentage point reductions in related
rates. In addition, the directors of the Boston, New York, and Dallas
Reserve Banks had voted to maintain their existing schedules of rates.

     The Board's discussion disclosed agreement that recent developments
in money and credit markets did not warrant a reduction in the discount rate
at this time, although a lower rate might be appropriate in the near future.
Consequently, the Board voted unanimously to <u>defer</u> action on the pending
discount rate requests.   (Participating in this discussion: Vice Chairman
Martin and Governors Wallich, Partee, Teeters, Rice, and Gramley.)

1

8/13/82 FOI copy

Discount rates. At its meeting on August 9, 1982, the Board
discussed but deferred action on requests by the directors of the
Federal Reserve Banks of Philadelphia, Atlanta, and Chicago to
establish a basic discount rate of 10-1/2 percent (a decrease from
11 percent), with corresponding 1/2 percentage point decreases in
related rates. In a memorandum dated August 13, 1982, the Office of
the Secretary reported that those requests were still pending and
that, subject to review and determination by the Board of Governors,
the directors of the Federal Reserve Banks of Minneapolis, Kansas
City, and Dallas had voted on August 12 to establish a basic rate of
10-1/2 percent, with corresponding 1/2 percentage point decreases in
related rates, while the directors of the San Francisco Bank had
voted to establish a basic rate of 10 percent, with corresponding
1 percentage point decreases in related rates. The remaining five
Banks had voted to maintain their existing schedules of rates.

At today's meeting, the Board considered recent economic and
financial developments. It was noted that loan demand at banks had
weakened recently and growth in the money supply continued to be
restrained. In addition, short-term market rates of interest had
declined. The Board's discussion of these factors disclosed agreement
that a reduction of 1/2 percentage point in the discount rate would be
appropriate.

8/13/82

Thereupon, the Board unanimously approved a reduction in the basic discount rate from 11 percent to 10-1/2 percent, with corresponding 1/2 percentage point decreases in related rates, effective August 16, 1982, for the six Banks that had established such rates. (Voting for this action. Chairman Volcker and Governors Martin, Wallich, Partee, Rice, and Gramley.)

The Board authorized issuance of a press release announcing its action. In addition, the Secretary of the Board was authorized to inform any other Reserve Bank that established a basic discount rate of 10-1/2 percent, along with appropriate related rates, of the Board's approval of that schedule of rates.

(Note: Subsequently, advice was received that the directors of the following Reserve Banks had established the lower rate schedule and those Banks were informed of the Board's approval, effective August 16:   Boston, New York, Cleveland, Richmond, St. Louis, and San Francisco.)

1

8/23/82   FOI copy

     <u>Discount rates</u>. In memorandum dated August 20, 1982,
the Office of the Secretary reported that, subject to review and
determination by the Board of Governors, the directors of the Federal
Reserve Banks of Philadelphia and Chicago on August 19, and the
Federal Reserve Bank of Atlanta on August 20, 1982, had voted to
establish a basic discount rate of 10 percent (a reduction from
10-1/2 percent), with corresponding 1/2 percentage point reductions in
related rates. The directors of the Boston and New York Reserve Banks
had voted to maintain their existing schedules of rates.

     The Board's consideration of the requests today disclosed
agreement that the discount rate should not be reduced at this time,
although recent economic and financial developments suggested that a
reduction might be appropriate in the near future. Thereupon, the
Board voted unanimously to <u>defer</u> action on the pending discount rate
requests. (Participating in this discussion: Chairman Volcker and
Governors Martin, Wallich, Partee, Teeters, and Rice.)

8/26/82

<u>Discount rates</u>. At its meeting on August 23, 1982, the Board

considered but deferred request from the directors of the

Federal Reserve Banks of Philadelphia, Atlanta, and Chicago to lower

the basic discount rate from 10-1/2 percent to 10 percent, with

corresponding 1/2 percentage point decreases in related rates. In a

memorandum dated August, 26, 1982, the Office of the Secretary reported

that those requests were still pending and that, subject to review and

determination by the Board of Governors, the directors of the Federal

Reserve Banks of St. Louis (on August 25), New York, Minneapolis,

Kansas City, and San Francisco (on August 26) also had voted to

establish the lower schedule of rates. The directors of the Federal

Reserve Banks of Boston, Cleveland, Richmond, and Dallas had voted to

maintain existing rates.

At today's meeting, the Board considered recent economic and

financial developments. Interest rates, especially short-term market

rates, had declined appreciably since a reduction of 1/2 percentage

point was approved on August 13, and the Board agreed that a further

1/2 percentage point reduction would be appropriate to bring the

discount rate into better alignment with those rates.

Thereupon, the Board unanimously <u>approved</u> a reduction in the

basic discount rate from 10-1/2 percent to 10 percent, with

corresponding 1/2 percentage point decreases in related rates,

effective August 27, 1982, for the eight Banks that had established

2

8/26/82   FOI copy

such rates. (Voting for this action: Chairman Volcker and Governors Martin, Wallich, and Partee.)

The Board <u>authorized</u> issuance of a press release regarding this action. In addition, the Secretary of the Board was <u>authorized</u> to inform any other Bank that established a basic rate of 10 percent, along with appropriate related rates, of the Board's approval of that schedule of rates.

(Note: Subsequently, advice was received that the directors of the following Reserve Banks had established the lower rate schedule, and those Banks were informed of the Board's approval, effective as indicated: Boston, Richmond, and Dallas, effective August 27; and Cleveland, effective August 30, 1982.)

Appendix II

Calculating "cone" and "tunnel" growth rates for the M-1 aggregate

Annual Fed target: 4–7%
(Fourth Quarter 1984–Fourth Quarter 1985)

Cone

1. Calculate base. Fourth quarter 1984 average for M-1 is $553.5 billion. Plot in November 1984.

2. Compute monthly lower and upper limits for the cone.

   $553.5 billon x 1.04 = $575.6 billion (lower)
   $553.5 billon x 1.07 = $592.2 billion (upper)

3. To derive *weekly* lower and upper M-1 *levels* for cone:

   $553.5 billion x .04 x n/52 = lower level

   $553.5 billion x .07 x n/52 = upper level

   where: n is the number of weeks into the measurement period starting with the week of November 13, 1984. Ideally, this week should be as close as possible to the exact mid-point of the fourth quarter base period.

Tunnel

1. Start again with the fourth quarter 1984 base of $553.5 billion.
2. Calculate monthly lower-, mid-, and upper ranges for M-1 growth through fourth quarter 1985.

   $553.5 billion x 1.04   = $575.6 billion (lower)
   $553.5 billion x 1.055 = $583.9 billion (mid)
   $553.5 billion x 1.07   = $592.2 billion (upper)
3. Subtract lower (575.6) from mid (583.9) = $8.3 billion and subtract mid (583.9) from upper (592.2) = $8.3 billion.
4. To derive the lower limit of the tunnel base, *subtract* $8.3 billion from fourth quarter base (553.5) which equals *$545.2 billion.*
5. To derive the upper limit of the tunnel base, *add* $8.3 billion to fourth quarter base (553.5) which equals *$561.8 billion.* Plot in November 1985.
6. To derive *weekly* upper and lower levels for the tunnel, subtract the tunnel base (545.2) from the tunnel terminal point (575.6) for the lower 4% growth path, which equals $30.4 billion then subtract the tunnel base (561.8) from the tunnel terminal point (592.2) for upper 7% growth path, which also equals $30.4 billion. To compute weekly M-1 levels.

   $30.4 billion x n/52 = lower level
   $30.4 billion x n/52 = upper level

   where: n is the number of weeks into the measurement period starting with the week of November 13, 1984. Ideally, this week should be as close as possible to the exact mid-point of the fourth quarter base period.

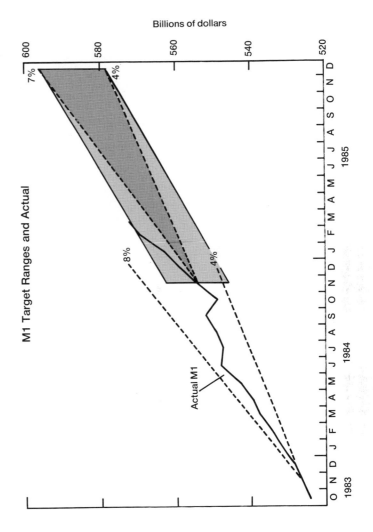

M1 Target Ranges and Actual

Billions of dollars

600
580
560
540
520

7%
4%
8%
4%
Actual M1

O N D J F M A M J J A S O N D J F M A M J J A S O N D
1983   1984   1985

153

Appendix III

*L*etter on "report on the conduct of monetary policy"

BOARD OF GOVERNORS

of the

FEDERAL RESERVE SYSTEM

WASHINGTON, D.C. 20551

November 6, 1985

PAUL A. VOLCKER

Chairman

The Honorable Walter E. Fauntroy
Chairman
Subcommittee on Domestic Monetary Policy
Committee on Banking, Finance and
    Urban Affairs
House of Representatives
Washington, D.C.   20515

Dear Walter:

On behalf of the other members of the Federal Reserve
Board and the Federal Open Market Committee, I want to thank you
for sending us your "Report on the Conduct of Monetary Policy."
Clearly, we are in broad agreement on the essential elements of
the current economic situation--including the consequences of
continued large federal budget deficits, which, through their
effects on the dollar and interest rates, have contributed to
the severe imbalance of our transactions with other countries
and the uneven performance of various sectors of our economy.
Given our common analysis of the economy, it is perhaps not
surprising that the Report supported the general conduct of
monetary policy over the first half of the year, when in the
face of falling velocity, narrow money grew at a rate well in
excess of the FOMC's objective for the year

With respect to the FOMC's policy objectives after
mid-year, the Report expresses concern about the appropriate
treatment of M1 in the implementation of policy. Specifically,
it proposes "downgrading" this aggregate, designating it as a
monitoring variable rather than an objective, and questions the
implications of the "rebasing" procedure adopted by the Open
Market Committee in July.

The FOMC's decision to rebase was made in the expectation that velocity behavior would be closer to historic patterns
in the second half of the year. The retention of M1 as an
intermediate objective for monetary policy reflected this expectation, along with the recognition that, historically, broad
movements in this aggregate have had a reasonably predictable
relationship to the ultimate objectives for policy in terms of
prices and spending.

As a practical matter, however, the velocity of M1
continued to decline over the summer, continuing the unusual

The Honorable Walter E. Fauntroy
Page Two

pattern of the earlier part of the year. In the light of the
current uncertainties surrounding the relationship of M1 to
economic activity and prices, the FOMC, as I suggested in my
testimony, has continued since mid-year to evaluate the behavior
of M1, and the broader aggregates as well, against the background of incoming information on the economy and developments
in foreign exchange and domestic credit markets. In fact, M1
growth in the third quarter was well in excess of the FOMC's
rebased target. That, in itself, has been a matter of concern,
but in light of continued declines in M1 velocity, growth in
broader monetary aggregates generally within longer-term ranges,
and the relatively high foreign exchange value of the dollar,
the Committee chose not to move aggressively to tighten reserve
availability to constrain M1 growth.

Slower growth in M1 is anticipated over the fourth
quarter as a whole, consistent with a probable small decline in
October. However, in the light of all the circumstances alluded
to earlier, the Committee has agreed that growth of M1 over the
second half of the year as a whole above the target range established in July would be acceptable. The target ranges for the
broader monetary aggregates remain appropriate.

Beyond the treatment of the monetary aggregates, your
Report made several recommendations concerning possible Federal
Reserve actions to address sectoral problems in the economy.
One was to renew the temporary seasonal program for discount
window loans to agricultural banks. As you may be aware, this
program got very little use this year, in part because our
modification of the regular seasonal program made that more
attractive, and in part because liquidity apparently was in
reasonably ample supply at agricultural banks. We will review
both the special temporary and regular seasonal programs over
the winter.

Another of the Report's recommendations was to study,
along with the Treasury Depaartment, ways to encourage lending in
support of "the most modern technologies." In general, as you
know, I am skeptical of the usefulness of such an approach. It
is not clear to me that spending for modern technology is being
constrained unduly by a shortage of funds. Moreover, I would
doubt whether government employees--at the Federal Reserve or
elsewhere--could discriminate adequately among competing technologies to determine which were especially deserving of more
funds than could be raised through normal private channels. In
addition, we have to recognize that directing funds into one

The Honorable Walter E. Fauntroy
Page Three

area inevitably leads, given the limited volume of savings in
our society, to less lending and spending in another area, which
is impossible to identify but could have an equally high
economic or social priority. Finally, I view Federal Reserve
involvement in credit allocation efforts as usually outside of,
and in some degree potentially inimical to, our responsibilities
to assess the overall adequacy of growth in money and credit to
support economic growth and price stability.

          I appreciate having the opportunity to comment on the
Report's recommendations.

                              Sincerely,

                              [SIGNATURE]

How to read
the official
FOMC policy record

There is no single more informative Fed document than the record of the Federal Open Market Committee (FOMC) policy actions.
It is a reasonably up-to-date Fed assessment of the economic outlook, monetary growth and possible Fed policy responses. The Fed makes the record for each FOMC meeting available to the public with a delay of 5–6 weeks. Specifically, the FOMC record for a given meeting is typically made available a few days after the next regularly scheduled FOMC meeting.

To provide some hints for the first-time readers of this must-document for Fed watchers, the record of policy actions of the FOMC at a typical meeting—the meeting on August 20, 1985—is reproduced in its entirety below. The sections of this document that Fed watchers should scrutinize are highlighted, along with some related marginal comments.

FEDERAL RESERVE press release

For Use at 4:30 p.m.

October 4, 1985

       The Federal Reserve Board and the Federal Open Market Committee today released the attached record of policy actions taken by the Federal Open Market Committee at its meeting on August 20, 1985.

       Such records for each meeting of the Committee are made available a few days after the next regularly scheduled meeting and are published in the Federal Reserve Bulletin and the Board's Annual Report. The summary descriptions of economic and financial conditions they contain are based solely on the information that was available to the Committee at the time of the meeting.

Attachment

1. This particular record of FOMC policy actions for the August 20, 1985 meeting was released on Friday October 4. This was three days after the regularly scheduled October 1, 1985 FOMC meeting.

RECORD OF POLICY ACTIONS OF THE

FEDERAL OPEN MARKET COMMITTEE

Meeting held on August 20, 1985

Domestic policy directive

The information reviewed at this meeting suggested that economic activity was probably expanding in the current quarter at a moderately faster pace than in the first half of the year. Broad measures of prices and wages continued to indicate that inflation was running at about the same pace as in 1984.

The index of industrial production rose 0.2 percent in July, about the same increase as in each of the preceding two months. Output of consumer goods was relatively strong, reflecting gains in the production of automobiles and home goods. Production of construction supplies and of materials also increased in July; but production of business equipment fell, and output of defense and space equipment declined after several months of extraordinarily rapid growth. Capacity utilization for total industry was 80.8 percent in July, unchanged since April and 1.2 percentage points below its year-earlier level.

Total nonfarm payroll employment rose 240,000 in July, a little above the average monthly increase during the first half of the year. Job gains remained uneven across industries, as employment in manufacturing declined slightly further while employment in service-producing industries continued to account for the bulk of the advance. The civilian unemployment rate remained at 7.3 percent in July, unchanged since February.

2. This moderate acceleration in economic activity in the third quarter of 1985 was welcomed since it followed a dismally slow 1.1.% average pace of real GNP growth in the first two quarters of the year.

The nominal value of retail sales increased 0.4 percent in July after two months of decline. Sales of general merchandise recovered somewhat after falling in May and June, and sales of furniture and appliances rose at about the average pace of the preceding two months. In the automotive sector, however, sales of domestic automobiles dropped to an annual rate of 7-1/2 million units--1 million below the average level earlier in the year when foreign cars were in short supply and financing incentive programs for domestic cars were prevalent. Sales slipped still further in early August to an annual rate of around 7 million units, with some of the slowing perhaps attributable to the recent strike by auto-haulers. The tentative settlement of that strike and the reintroduction of below-market-rate financing programs pointed to a likely rebound in sales of domestically produced autos.

Total private housing starts fell slightly in July to an annual rate of 1.65 million units. The lower pace reflected a drop in starts of multifamily units, as starts of single-family structures edged higher. Other indicators suggested some pickup in construction activity in the near term: newly issued permits for residential building remained at a high level relative to starts, consumer attitudes toward buying houses were quite positive, and informal trade reports from homebuilders indicated heightened buyer interest and sales activity.

Trends in business capital spending have been obscured lately by extreme volatility in monthly data, but available information suggested further growth over the period ahead, though probably at a relatively modest

3. The economic statistics recited on pages 1, 2, and 3 of this August policy record don't deserve much attention. The only point to look for is whether the economic data are following a pattern in line with Fed expectations.

pace, following the extraordinarily rapid growth earlier in the economic

expansion. In June, the latest month for which data on business investment

were available, new orders and shipments of nondefense capital goods rebounded.

On the other hand, outlays for nonresidential construction weakened.

　　　　The producer price index for finished goods rose 0.3 percent in

July, after declining 0.2 percent in June. The rise in July reflected in

part a surge in prices of fresh vegetables that boosted the index for

finished foods 1.3 percent; other food prices generally declined, however,

and prices of crude foods fell in July for the seventh consecutive month.

The consumer price index rose 0.2 percent in June, the same as in May.

Food prices changed little over the two-month period and consumer commodity

prices declined, but service prices continued to rise at a comparatively

rapid rate. Thus far in 1985, producer and consumer prices and the index

of average hourly earnings had risen at rates close to those recorded

in 1984.

　　　　Since the committee's meeting in July, the trade-weighted value

of the dollar against major foreign currencies had fallen nearly 4-3/4 per-

cent further, to a level about 17 percent below its peak in late February.

Most of the recent decline was in the early part of the intermeeting period;

since late July the dollar's value had declined only slightly further on

balance. The U.S. merchandise trade deficit widened in the second quarter

to a record annual rate of nearly $134 billion. Both agricultural and non-

agricultural exports fell substantially, while imports registered a small

increase. The rise in imports was attributable to a substantial increase

in the volume of oil imports after a sharp decline in the first quarter.

At its meeting on July 9-10, 1985, the Committee had adopted
a directive that called for maintaining the existing degree of pressures
on reserve positions, keeping in mind the possibility of some increase in
those pressures if growth of the monetary aggregates exceeded intentions.
That action was expected to be consistent with growth of both M2 and M3
at an annual rate of around 7-1/2 percent for the period from June to
September. Over the same period the expansion of M1 was expected to slow
substantially to an annual rate of 5 to 6 percent. The members agreed
that somewhat lesser restraint on reserve positions might be acceptable
in the event of growth in the monetary aggregates that was substantially
slower than expected while somewhat greater restraint would be acceptable
if monetary growth were substantially faster. In either case, adjustments
in the degree of reserve pressures would be considered against the background of developments relating to the strength of the business expansion,
progress against inflation, and conditions in domestic credit and foreign
exchange markets. The intermeeting range for the federal funds rate was
retained at 6 to 10 percent.

Though slowing from the quite rapid May-June pace, M1 had shown
relatively strong growth since midyear; it increased at an annual rate of
about 9 percent in July and data for early August indicated the likelihood
of stronger growth in the current month. Thus, its expansion appeared to
be well above the Committee's expectations for the June-to-September period.
The strength in M1 reflected an acceleration in other checkable deposits
while demand deposits, though increasing little on balance, remained at
high levels as the extraordinary surge of late spring in such deposits
showed no signs of unwinding. Expansion in the broader aggregates slowed

**4. This section of the policy record, which discusses developments since
the preceding FOMC meeting, is extremely important. Note that there is
a subtle but significant difference in wording at the July 9-10, 1985 meeting. The wording difference suggests that Fed policy-makers "would be"
more willing to tighten reserve pressures than to ease them.**

in July from the average pace over the previous two months, to annual rates
of about 8-1/2 percent for M2 and 4-1/4 percent for M3. For the period
from the fourth quarter of 1984 through July, growth in M2 was around the
upper end of its range for 1985, while the recent sluggish growth in M3
had brought its growth to around the midpoint of its range. Expansion in
total domestic nonfinancial debt remained high relative to the Committee's
monitoring range for the year.

Early in the intermeeting interval open market operations were
directed at maintaining the existing degree of pressures on reserves. By
early August, with M1 running well above the Committee's expectations at the
time of the July meeting, and with M2 also on the high side, against the
background of a weaker dollar and sustained economic activity, desk operations
were conducted with a view toward more cautious provision of reserves. The
level of adjustment plus seasonal borrowing, which had been artificially high
around the time of the July meeting because of seasonal strains associated
with the midyear statement date and July 4 holiday period, averaged about
$410 million in the two-week maintenance period ending July 31 and rose to
$480 million in the first half of August.

The weekly average federal funds rate was generally in the 7-3/4
to 7-7/8 percent area during the intermeeting interval, though average
daily rates ranged from about 7-3/8 percent to as high as 8-3/4 percent.
Most other short-term interest rates rose about 20 to 45 basis points over
the intermeeting interval, mainly reflecting a reassessment by market participants of the outlook for the economy and for monetary policy. Yields
on intermediate- and long-term Treasury securities increased about 20 to 30

**5. This key reference confirms that Fed policy-makers moved in early-Au-
gust (before the regularly scheduled August 20 meeting) to tighten reserve
pressures. The Fed tightened reserve pressures primarily in response to
excessive M-1 growth. Note also that although the Fed doesn't reveal the
precise level for its borrowing target, it hints that the move to tighten
was accompanied by an increase in the Fed's operating target for adjustment plus seasonal borrowing to perhaps $450-500 million from $400-450
million.**

basis points, while yields on corporate bonds generally rose somewhat more. The average contract rate on new commitments for fixed-rate conventional home mortgage loans moved up slightly to around 12-1/4 percent.

The staff projections presented at this meeting suggested that growth in real GNP would pick up somewhat in the second half of the year from the sluggish pace in the first half, and would continue at a modest pace through 1986. Although domestic final demand was projected to rise less rapidly than earlier this year, a larger share of the increase was expected to be met out of domestic production rather than from imports or reduced inventory investment. The unemployment rate was projected to edge down only slightly over the forecast horizon and the rate of increase in prices was projected to remain close to that experienced in recent years.

In the Committee's discussion of the economic situation and outlook, the members focused on various uncertainties and risks inherent in current economic and financial conditions. They noted with some concern the absence of clear evidence that business activity might be strengthening, as they had expected earlier, following sluggish growth during the first half of 1985. Nonetheless, with domestic final demands remaining relatively buoyant, most of the members agreed that some pickup in the rate of economic expansion continued to be reasonable expectation for the second half of the year. They recognized that various imbalances and financial strains in the economy constituted ongoing threats to the economic expansion and raised the danger that growth would be more sluggish than anticipated. Some members also observed that unexpected developments stemming from domestic or international financial problems or from other difficulties in specific sectors of the

6. The Committee's view of the economic situation and outlook is more important than the FOMC staff projections. On balance, the committee seemed fairly positive towards the near-term economic outlook.

economy, if not contained, could interrupt the expansion itself. On the other hand, a few members remained relatively optimistic about the prospective performance of the eocnomy; it was also suggsted that the rapid growth in M1 in recent months might well lead with some lag to faster economic expansion than was currently anticipated.

Particular emphasis was given during the Committee's discussion to the prospect that domestic economic developments would depend importantly on international conditions, including the economic performance of industrialized countries, the ability and willingness of developing countries to manage their foreign debt problems, the global energy situation, and the foreign exchange value of the dollar. The members continued to stress, as they had at previous meetings, the strongly adverse impact that foreign competition, fostered by a high value of the dollar in foreign exchange markets, was having on overall domestic economic activity and in particular on many manufacturing firms and on agriculture. Some members commented that the prospects for near-term improvement in the balance of trade seemed to be relatively remote.

While a further decline in the dollar would tend with some lag to have a favorable impact on the balance of trade, a sense of "free fall" in the dollar would represent a major threat to progress toward price stability and interest rates. In general, while a decline over time would not be disturbing, it was viewed as important to maintain a certain confidence in the dollar, given the large net inflows of funds from abroad needed to bridge the gap between the relatively limited availability of domestic saving and the funds required to finance the federal budget deficit and private capital

7. The fed placed more emphasis than usual on the dollar in its August policy deliberations. The monetary authorities seemed to be intent on avoiding a "free-fall" in the value of the dollar in terms of major foreign currencies.

167

outlays. Without provision of such funds relatively willingly from abroad,
pressures on domestic interest rates would be greater than otherwise. The
members agreed that the transition to a lower trade deficit and a more sustainable pattern of international transactions generally, presumably accompanied
by a lower dollar, would be greatly facilitated by substantial progress in
reducing future deficits in the federal budget and by the avoidance of protectionist legislation that could have a highly unfavorable effect on international trade, on the ability of developing countries to resolve their external debt problems, and on the overall performance of the domestic economy.
Several members noted that the risks associated with the underlying distortions and problems in the domestic economy and the persisting strains in
domestic and international financial markets posed dilemmas that were not
amenable to a monetary policy solution.

As they had at earlier meetings, the members commented on the
uneven pattern of developments in various sectors of the economy. They
gave special emphasis to the problems in agriculture but also cited other
problem or lagging areas of the economy. In most parts of the country,
however, strength in a number of industries such as services and defense
production currently tended to outweigh the economic weaknesses. In the
construction area, one member called attention to recent indications of
reduced nonresidential building activity and other members commented that
vacancy rates in office structures were relatively high in several parts
of the country. On the other hand, there were reports of growing buyer
interest in housing, although recent data on housing starts were weaker
than expected. With regard to financial conditions, a number of members
referred to various financial practices and the buildup or incautious use
of debt that had rendered many borrowers and their lenders more vulnerable

to economic adversity. In the case of consumers, rising debt burdens

together with the possibility of reduced income growth were viewed by at

least some members as likely to restrain expansion in consumer expenditures.

At its meeting in July the Committee had reviewed the basic policy

objectives that it had established in February for growth of the monetary and

credit aggregates in 1985 and had set tentative objectives for expansion in 1986.

For the period from the fourth quarter of 1984 to the fourth quarter of 1985,

the Committee had reaffirmed the ranges for the broader aggregates set in

February of 6 to 9 percent for M2 and 6 to 9-1/2 percent for M3. The associated

range for total domestic nonfinancial debt was also reaffirmed at 9 to 12 per-

cent for 1985. With respect to M1, the base was moved forward to the second

quarter of 1985 and a range of 3 to 8 percent at an annual growth rate was

established for the period to the fourth quarter of the year. For 1986 the

Committee agreed on tentative monetary growth objectives that included re-

ductions of 1 percentage point in the upper end of the M1 range and 1/2 per

centage point in the upper end of the M3 range. The provisional range for

total domestic nonfinancial debt was reduced by 1 percentage point for 1986.

In the Committee's discussion of policy implementation for the weeks

immediately ahead, the members took particular account of the disparate behavior

of M1 and the economy. Under the circumstances, a consensus emerged against

making a substantial change for the time being in the degree of reserve restraint

that had been sought recently. The members recognized that the behavior of M1

was subject to unpredictable fluctuations. Nonetheless, they continued to

expect that the expansion in M1 would moderate appreciably over the months

ahead, if something like the current degree of restraint on reserve positions

was maintained.

**8. This is always an important section in its discussion of policy im-
plementation for the weeks beyond the August 20 meeting, the FOMC
decided against making a substantial change in reserve pressures. Instead,
Fed policy-makers decided to maintain the slightly greater degree of
reserve restraint sought recently.**

169

In the course of the Committee's discussion, a number of members
emphasized the uncertainties surrounding the behavior of M1 and the downside
risks they saw in the economy. Under prevailing circumstances, the surge
in M1 growth might not have the usual inflationary implications. The
demand for assets in M1 appeared to have been influenced by the relatively
low level of interest rates on market instruments and also on small time
certificates of deposits, and the velocity of money seemed to be continuing
to decline sharply. Moreover, there had been no signs of increasing price
pressures in aggregate price indicators or in commodity markets. It was
also argued that the objective of achieving M1 growth within the Committee's
long-run range might receive somewhat reduced emphasis, at least for a
time, pending evaluation of further developments including the performance
of the broader aggregates.

Other members expressed more concern that further M1 growth at rates
substantially above the Committee's long-run range would have inflationary
consequences over time. They noted the persisting strength of M1 in recent
weeks, and should that continue, they felt that added reserve restraint
would probably be desirable to bring M1 closer to the upper end, or within,
the Committee's long-run range by the fourth quarter. Continued strength
in M1 could also raise questions about the Committee's commitment to an
anti-inflationary policy, with potentially adverse implications for inflationary expectations. Some members also commented that the rapid growth in
M1 had already built up considerable liquidity that would tend to sustain
·the expansion over the months ahead.

While there were shadings of opinion with regard to the appropriate degree of reserve pressure under the circumstances, on balance a majority of the members indicated their acceptance of a directive that called for maintaining the slightly firmer degree of reserve restraint that had been sought in recent weeks. The members expected such an approach to policy implementation to be consistent with growth of M2 and M3 at annual rates of around 8-1/2 and 6-1/2 percent respectively for the period from June to September, not much changed from expectations at the time of the July meeting. Growth in M1 was expected to slow from its recent pace, but given the rapid expansion since June, M1 was now anticipated to grow at an annual rate of about 8 to 9 percent over the three-month period, considerably above earlier expectations. Two members argued for immediate adjustments in the degree of reserve pressures -- although in opposing directions -- based on their differing evaluations of the significance of recent monetary growth for inflation and economic activity as against the risks to sustained expansion stemming from the financial vulnerabilities and the underlying imbalances in the economy.

In keeping with the Committee's usual practice, the members contemplated the possible need for some intermeeting adjustment in the degree of reserve restraint. They agreed that somewhat greater restraint on reserve positions would be acceptable if growth in the monetary aggregates were substantially faster than expected, while somewhat lesser restraint would be acceptable if monetary growth were substantially slower. As in the past, any such adjustment should not be made automatically in response to the behavior of the monetary aggregates alone, but should take broader economic and financial developments into account, including conditions in domestic

9. Always look for the policy conclusion of the "majority of members." Note also the Fed's intermediate targets, usually covering a three-month period, for M-1, M-2, and M-3 growth.

and international financial markets. For the period ahead, several members
believed that policy implementation should be especially alert to developments in the foreign exchange markets. The members agreed that the intermeeting range for the federal funds rate, which provides a mechanism for
initiating consultation of the Committee when its boundaries are persistently
exceeded, should be left unchanged at 6 to 10 percent.

At the conclusion of the meeting, the following domestic policy
directive was issued to the Federal Reserve Bank of New York:

> The information reviewed at this meeting suggests
> that economic activity is probably expanding in the
> current quarter at a moderately faster rate than in
> the first half of the year. In July, industrial
> production continued to move somewhat higher and
> total retail sales rose modestly after two months
> of decline. On the other hand, housing starts fell
> somewhat in July. Information on business capital
> spending suggests further growth, though at a much
> less rapid pace than earlier in the economic ex-
> pansion. Total nonfarm payroll employment continued
> to increase in July, although employment in manu-
> facturing declined slightly further. The civilian
> unemployment rate remained at 7.3 percent in July,
> unchanged since February. Broad measures of prices
> and wages appear to be rising at rates close to
> those recorded in 1984.
>
> Since the Committee's meeting in July, the trade-
> weighted value of the dollar against major foreign
> currencies has depreciated further. The merchandise
> trade deficit widened in the second quarter to the
> highest rate on record. Both agricultural and non-
> agricultural exports fell substantially, while imports
> registered a small increase.
>
> Based on data for July and early August, M1 has
> been growing relatively rapidly. Demand deposits have
> shown little change on balance, but other checkable
> deposits have explained substantially. Growth in M2
> has continued at around the upper end of its 1985

range, while relatively sluggish growth in M3 recently
has brought this aggregate to the midpoint of its
range. Expansion in total domestic nonfinancial debt
has remained high relative to the Committee's monitoring
range for the year. Mosat interest rates have risen
somewhat since the July meeting of the Committee.

The Federal Open Market Committee seeks to foster
monetary and financial conditions that will help to
reduce inflation further, promote growth in output
on a sustainable basis, and contribute to an improved
pattern of international transactions. In furtherance
of these objectives the Committee at the July meeting
reaffirmed ranges for the year of 6 to 9 percent for
M2 and 6 to 9-1/2 percent for M3. The associated
range for total domestic nonfinancial debt was reaffirmed at 9 to 12 percent. With respect to M1,
the base was moved forward to the second quarter of
1985 and a range was established at an annual growth
rate of 3 to 8 percent. The range takes account of
expectations of a return of velocity growth toward
more usual patterns, following the sharp decline in
velocity during the first half of the year, while
also recognizing a higher degree of uncertainty
regarding that behavior. The appropriateness of
the new range will continue to be reexamined in
the light of evidence with respect to economic
and financial developments including developments
in foreign exchange markets. More generally, the
Committee agreed that growth in the aggregates may
be in the upper parts of their ranges, depending on
continuing developments with respect to velocity
and provided that inflationary pressures remain
subdued.

For 1986 the Committee agreed on tentative ranges
of monetary growth, measured from the fourth quarter
of 1985 to the fourth quarter of 1986, of 4 to 7 percent
for M1, 6 to 9 percent for M2, and 6 to 9 percent for
M3. The associated range for growth in total domestic
nonfinancial debt was provisionally set at 8 to 11
percent for 1986. With respect to M1 particularly,
the Committee recognized that uncertainties surrounding
recent behavior of velocity would require careful
reappraisel of the target range at the beginning of
1986. Moreover, in establishing ranges for next year,

the Committee also recongnized that account would need
to be taken of experience with institutional and
depositor behavior in response to the completion of
deposit rate deregulation early in the year.

In the implementation of policy for the immediate
future, the Committee seeks to maintain the degree of
pressure on reserve positions sought in recent weeks..
This action is expected to be consistent with growth
in M2 and M3 at annual rates of around 8-1/2 and 6-1/2
percent, respectively, during the period from June to
September. M1 growth is expected to slow from its
recent pace, but given the rapid growth in recent
weeks, expansion over the June-to-September period may
be at an 8 to 9 percent annual rate. Somewhat greater
restraint would be acceptable in the event of substantially higher growth in the monetary aggregates.
Somewhat lesser restraint would be acceptable in the
event of substantially slower growth. In either case
such a change would be considered in the context of
appraisals of the strength of the business expansion,
developments in foreign exchange markets, progress
against inflation, and conditions in domestic and
international credit markets. The Chairman may call
for Committee consultation if it appears to the
Manager for Domestic Operations that pursuit of the
monetary objectives and related reserve paths during
the period before the next meeting is likely to be
associated with a federal funds rate persistently
outside a range of 6 to 10 percent.

Votes for this section: Messrs. Volcker,
Corrigan, Balles, Forrestal, Keehn, Martin,
Partee, Rice, and Wallich. Votes against this
action: Mr. Black and Ms. Seger. (Absent
and not voting: Mr. Gramley.)

Mr. Black dissented because he preferred to direct open market

operations promptly toward a somewhat greater degree of reserve restraint

and thereby improve the prospects of moderating M1 growth to within the

Committee's range for the second half of the year. Ms. Seger dissented

because she favored some reduction in the degree of reserve restraint in

10. Formal statement of the Fed's policy stance is incorporated in this policy directive.

light of the financial vulnerability of some sectors of the economy and
in order to encourage sustained economic expansion.

At a telephone consultation on September 23, the Committee
discussed the possible implications for intervention in foreign exchange
markets of the deliberations during the weekend of the Ministers of
Finance and Central Bank Governors of the G-5 countries. In the
course of discussion, it was indicated that the likely potential for
U.S. sales of dollars and acquisitions of foreign currencies over the
near term fell generally within existing Committee authorization.

**11. Dissents can be important, though major internal policy splits are
rare.**

**12. This telephone consultation suggests that the Fed is giving consider-
able weight to the G-5 initiatives.**

Appendix V

*P*eriodic Federal Reserve releases

*Anticipated schedule of release dates for periodic releases—
Board of Governors of The Federal Reserve System[1]*

Weekly Releases	Approximate release days	Date or period to which data refer
Aggregate Reserves of Depository Institutions and Monetary Base. H.3 (502) [1.20]	Thursday	Week ended previous Wednesday
Actions of the Board; Applications and Reports. H.2 (501)	Friday	Week ended previous Saturday
Assets and Liabilities of Insured Domestically Chartered and Foreign Related Banking Institutions. H.8(510)[1.25]	Monday	Wednesday, 3 weeks earlier
Changes in State Member Banks. K.3 (615)	Tuesday	Week ended previous Saturday
Factors Affecting Reserves of Depository Institutions and Condition Statement of Federal Reserve Banks. H.4.1 (503) [1.11]	Thursday	Week ended previous Wednesday
Foreign Exchange Rates. H.10 (512) [3.28]	Monday	Week ended previous Friday
Money Stock, Liquid Assets, and Debit Measures. H.6 (508) [1.21]	Thursday	Week ended Wednesday of previous week
Selected Borrowings in Immediately Available Funds of Large Member Banks. H.5 (507) [1.13]	Wednesday	Week ended Thursday of previous week
Selected Interest Rates. H.15 (519) [1.35]	Monday	Week ended previous Saturday
Weekly Consolidated Condition Report of Large Commercial Banks and Domestic Subsidiaries. H.4.2 (504) [1.26, 1.28, 1.29, 1.30]	Friday	Wednesday, 1 week earlier

Monthly Releases

Release		
Capacity Utilization: Manufacturing, Mining, Utilities and Industrial Materials. G.3 (402) [2.12]	Midmonth	Previous month
Changes in Status of Banks and Branches. G.4.5 (404)	1st of month	Previous month
Commercial and Industrial Loan Commitments at Selected Large Commercial Banks. G.21 (423)	2nd week of month	2nd month previous
Consumer Installment Credit. G.19 (421) [1.55, 1.56]	Midmonth	2nd month previous
Debits and Deposit Turnover at Commercial Banks. G.6 (406) [1.22]	12th of month	Previous month
Finance Companies. G.20 (422) [1.51, 1.52]	5th working day of month	2nd month previous
Foreign Exchange Rates. G.5 (405) [3.28]	1st of month	Previous month
Industrial Production. G.12.3(414)[2.13]	Midmonth	Previous month
Loans and Securities at all Commercial Banks. G.7 (407) [1.23]	3rd week of month	Previous month
Major Nondeposit Funds of Commercial Banks. G.10 (411) [1.24]	3rd week of month	Previous month
Maturity Distribution of Outstanding Negotiable Time Certificates of Deposit at Large Commercial Banks. G.9(410)	3rd week of month	Last Wednesday of previous month
Monthly Report of Assets and Liabilities of International Banking Facilities. G.14 (416)	2nd week of month	Wednesday, 2 weeks earlier
Research Library–Recent Acquisitions. G.15 (417)	1st of month	Previous month

1. Release dates are those anticipated or usually met. However, please note that for some releases there is normally a certain variability because .of reporting or processing proceedures. Moreover, for all series unusual circumstances may, from time to time, result in a release date being later than anticipated.

The Federal Reserve *Bulletin* table that reports these data is designated in brackets.

179

Monthly Releases—Continued

	Approximate release days	*Date or period to which data refer*
Selected Interest Rates. G.13 (415) [1.35]	3rd working day of month	Previous month
Quarterly Releases		
Agricultural Finance Databook. E.15 (125)	End of March, June, September, and December	January, April, July, and October
Country Exposure Lending Survey. E.16 (126)	January, April, July, and October	Previous 3 months
Domestic Offices, Commercial Bank Assets and Liabilities Consolidated Report of Condition. E.3.4 (113) [1.26, 1.28]	March, June, September, and December	Previous 6 months
Flow of Funds: Seasonally adjusted and unadjusted. Z.1 (780) [1.58, 1.59]	23rd of February, May, August, and November	Previous quarter
Flow of Funds Summary Statistics Z.7. (788) [1.57, 1.58]	15th of February, May, August, and November	Previous quarter
Geographical Distribution of Assets and Liabilities of Major Foreign Branches of U.S. Banks. E.11 (121)	15th of March, June, September, and December	Previous quarter
Survey of Terms of Bank Lending. E.2 (111) [1.34]	Midmonth of March, June, September, and December	February, May, August, and November
List of OTC Margin Stocks. E.7 (117)	January, April, July, and October	February, May, August, and November
Annual Releases		
Aggregate Summaries of Annual Surveys of Security Credit Extension. C.2 (101)	February	End of previous June

*B*usiness cycle
expansions and contractions
in the United States

Business cycles reference dates		Duration in months			
				Cycle	
Trough	Peak	Contraction (trough from previous peak)	Expansion (trough to peak)	Trough from previous trough	Peak from previous peak
December 1854	June 1857	....	30	....	....
December 1858	October 1860	18	22	48	40
June 1861	April 1865	8	46	30	54
December 1867	June 1869	32	18	78	50
December 1870	October 1873	18	34	36	52
March 1879	March 1882	65	36	99	101
May 1885	March 1887	38	22	74	60
April 1888	July 1890	13	27	35	40
May 1891	January 1893	10	20	37	30
June 1894	December 1895	17	18	37	35
June 1897	June 1899	18	24	36	42
December 1900	September 1902	18	21	42	39
August 1904	May 1907	23	33	44	56
June 1908	January 1910	13	19	46	32
January 1912	January 1913	24	12	43	36
December 1914	August 1918	23	44	35	67
March 1919	January 1920	7	10	51	17
July 1921	May 1923	18	22	28	40
July 1924	October 1926	14	27	36	41
November 1927	August 1929	13	21	40	34

March 1933	May 1937	43	50	64	93
June 1938	February 1945	13	80	63	93
October 1945	November 1948	8	37	88	45
October 1949	July 1953	11	45	48	56
May 1954	August 1957	10	39	55	49
April 1958	April 1960	8	24	47	32
February 1961	December 1969	10	106	34	116
November 1970	November 1973	11	36	117	47
March 1975	January 1980	16	58	52	74
July 1980	July 1981	6	12	64	18
November 1982		16		28	
Average all cycles:					
1854-1982 (30 cycles)		18	33	51	'51
1854-1919 (16 cycles)		22	27	48	'49
1919-1945 (6 cycles)		18	35	53	53
1945-1982 (8 cycles)		11	45	56	55
Average peacetime cycle:					
1854-1982 (25 cycles)		19	27	46	46
1854-1919 (14 cycles)		22	24	46	47
1919-1945 (5 cycles)		20	26	46	45
1945-1982 (6 cycles)		11	34	46	44

'29 cycles   '15 cycles   '24 cycles   '13 cycles

NOTE: Underscored figures are the wartime expansions (Civil War, World Wars I and II, Korean War, and Vietnam War) the postwar contractions and the run cycles that include wartime expansions.

Source: National Bureau of Economic Research Inc.

*G*rowth of
major debt aggregates
by sector

December 6, 1985
nonfinancial debt

			Domestic nonfinancial sectors								Total Non-Finan-cial	Memo: Private Finan Assets
			Households			Nonfinancial business						
	Total	U.S. Govt.	Pvt. Nonfin	Total	Home Mtges	Consumer Credit	Total	Long Term	Short Term	State & Local Govts	Foreign		

Annual change (per cent)

	Total	U.S. Govt.	Pvt. Nonfin	Total	Home Mtges	Consumer Credit	Total	Long Term	Short Term	State & Local Govts	Foreign	Total Non-Finan-cial	Memo: Private Finan Assets
1973	10.7	2.4	12.7	12.9	12.9	13.5	14.2	10.4	21.8	7.1	10.5	10.7	11.3
1974	9.0	3.4	10.3	7.8	8.8	4.9	13.4	10.3	19.1	7.6	22.4	9.5	8.1
1975	9.2	23.7	6.1	7.2	8.8	4.5	5.3	9.2	-1.3	5.9	14.2	9.4	9.5
1976	10.7	15.5	9.5	11.7	12.6	11.4	8.4	8.9	7.4	6.0	21.2	11.1	10.5
1977	12.8	11.0	13.2	16.3	16.9	16.2	12.4	11.1	14.7	5.1	12.2	12.7	10.5
1978	13.1	9.4	14.0	17.0	17.5	16.9	12.8	10.5	17.1	6.7	27.2	13.6	11.0
1979	12.1	6.0	13.6	15.1	16.1	13.5	13.6	9.9	20.1	6.7	12.5	12.1	11.2
1980	9.5	11.9	9.0	8.9	11.4	1.2	9.7	8.7	11.2	6.2	14.9	9.8	9.4
1981	9.5	11.8	9.0	8.3	7.9	6.0	11.1	7.6	16.6	2.3	13.0	9.7	11.0
1982	9.2	19.4	6.8	5.6	4.8	4.5	7.6	7.1	8.3	8.5	6.6	9.1	9.9
1983	11.6	18.8	9.7	11.3	10.3	13.6	7.7	9.2	5.5	11.4	8.3	11.4	11.0
1984	14.7	16.9	14.0	13.0	11.1	20.0	15.4	13.2	18.7	12.2	1.1	14.1	14.1

Quarterly Growth Rates (%—SAAR)

1983—	I	9.8	21.1	6.7	7.8	7.0	6.9	5.7	8.4	1.8	6.8	4.0	9.5	10.3
	II	11.6	22.4	8.5	10.4	9.7	11.1	5.5	9.0	.3	14.8	9.5	11.5	11.9
	III	11.1	15.0	10.0	12.0	11.6	13.4	8.2	9.6	5.9	9.3	5.6	10.9	11.5
	IV	12.0	12.0	12.1	13.3	11.6	20.5	10.6	8.7	13.5	12.9	13.3	12.1	11.1
1984—	I	12.9	14.7	12.3	11.2	10.5	16.9	14.6	9.5	22.3	6.5	-2.7	12.2	12.2
	II	14.0	14.0	14.0	14.0	11.9	23.4	15.7	12.3	20.6	5.0	21.6	14.3	14.5
	III	12.7	15.4	11.9	11.2	10.1	17.0	12.3	12.9	11.4	14.0	-15.0	11.5	11.9
	IV	16.1	19.5	15.1	13.2	10.3	17.3	15.8	15.6	16.0	21.5	1.5	15.5	15.2
1985—	I	11.5	10.6	11.8	12.2	9.5	20.9	10.7	12.0	8.9	14.8	-2.9	10.9	11.0
	II	12.7	15.7	11.8	12.5	10.7	17.8	9.7	13.3	4.4	19.2	1.0	12.3	10.4
	III	12.6	11.4	13.0	14.0	12.3	17.9	9.5	12.1	5.5	26.0	2.6	12.3	11.6
	IV	19.2	23.7	17.9	15.6	12.3	11.6	12.7	15.0	9.1	53.4	-1.3	18.5	16.2

Appendix VIII

Schedule of release dates for principal Federal economic indicators for 1986

Schedule of release dates for principal federal economic indicators for 1986

BUREAU OF THE CENSUS

	Jan	Feb	Mar	Apr	May	June	July	Aug	Sept	Oct	Nov	Dec
Value of New Construction Put in Place	2	3	3	1	1	2	1	1	2	1	3	1
				Data are for second month previous								
Housing Starts and Building Permits	17	19	18	16	16	17	17	20	17	17	19	16
			Data are for previous month									
New One Family Houses Sold and For Sale	31	—	5 / 31	29	30	30	30	29	30	30	—	3 / 30
		Data generally are for previous month										
Wholesale Trade	9	10	12	8	7	9	9	7	9	8	7	11
			Data are for second month previous									
Advance Retail Sales	14	13	13	11	13	12	15	13	12	15	14	11
			Data are for previous month									

Report												
Advance Report of U.S. Merchandise Trade	30	28	27	30	30	27	30	29	30	30	26	31
Data are for previous month												
Manufacturing and Trade Inventories and Sales	15	**14**	14	14	14	13	16	14	15	16	17	12
Data for second month previous												
Manufacturers Shipments Inventories and Orders	2	3	5	1/30	—	2	2/31	—	2	1/31	—	4
Data generally are for second month previous												
Advance Report Manufacturers' Shipments and Orders	24	25	22	22	24	23	22	23	23	25	23	
Data are for previous month												
Quarterly Financial Report–Manufacturing, Mining, and Wholesale Trade	7 (3Q'85)	7 (4Q'85)	16 (1Q'86)	15 (2Q'86)	15 (3Q'86)							
Reference period shown in parenthesis												
Quarterly Financial Report–Retail	15 (3Q'85)	7 (4Q'85)	16 (1Q'86)	8 (2Q'86)								
Reference period shown in parenthesis												
Housing Vacancies	29	25	28	28								
Data refer to previous quarter												

191

BUREAU OF ECONOMIC ANALYSIS

	Jan	Feb	Mar	Apr	May	June	July	Aug	Sept	Oct	Nov	Dec
Personal Income and Outlays	23	21	20	18	21	19	23	20	19	22	20	18
Data are for previous month												
Composite Indexes of Leading, Coincident, and Lagging Indicators	30	—	4 / 28	29	29	—	1 / 31	28	30	31	—	2 / 30
Data generally are for previous month												
Gross National Product	22	20	19	17	20	18	22	19	18	21	19	17
	(4Q'85)	(4Q'85)	(4Q'85)	(1Q'86)	(1Q'86)	(1Q'86)	(2Q'86)	(2Q'86)	(2Q'86)	(3Q'86)	(3Q'86)	(3Q'86)
Preliminary, 1st revision, 2nd revision estimates are issued for each quarter												
Corporate Profits	—	—	19	17	20	18	—	19	18	—	19	17
			(4Q'85)	(4Q'85)	(1Q'86)	(1Q'86)		(2Q'86)	(2Q'86)		(3Q'86)	(3Q'86)
Preliminary and revised estimates are issued for each quarter												
Plant and Equipment Expenditures	—	—	10	—	—	12	—	—	11	—	—	18
Data generally refer to previous quarter												
Merchandise Trade, Balance of Payments Basis	—	12	—	—	11	—	—	—	10	—	—	10
Data refer to previous quarter												

Summary of International Transactions	—	18	—	17	—	—	—	16	—	—	16
	Data are for previous quarter										
BUREAU OF LABOR STATISTICS											
The Employment Situation	8	7	7	4	6	3	1	5	3	7	5
	Data are for previous month										
Consumer Price Index	22	25	25	22	20	23	21	23	23	25	19
	Data are for previous month										
Product Price Indexes	10	14	14	11	13	11	15	12	10	14	12
	Data are for previous month										
Real Earnings	22	25	25	22	20	23	21	23	23	25	19
	Data are for previous month										
Productivity and Costs	29	27	—	24	—	29	26	—	28	—	1
	Data are for previous quarter										

BUREAU OF LABOR STATISTICS-Continued

	Jan	Feb	Mar	Apr	May	June	July	Aug	Sept	Oct	Nov	Dec
Major Collective Bargaining Settlements in Private Industry	27	—	—	25	—	—	28	—	—	27	—	—
	Data are for previous quarter											
Employment Cost Index	28	—	—	29	—	—	29	—	—	28	—	—
	Data are for previous quarter											
U.S. Import and Export Price Indexes	30	—	—	—	1	—	31	—	—	30	—	—
	Data are for previous quarter											

FEDERAL RESERVE BOARD

Money Stock, Liquid Assets, and Debt Measures

Data are issued every Thursday for the week ended Wednesday of previous week[1]

Factors Affecting Reserves of Depository Institutions and Condition Statement of Federal Reserve Banks

Data are issued every Thursday for the week ended previous Wednesday[1]

Consolidated Condition Report of Large Commercial Banks and Domestic Subsidiaries

Data are issued every Friday for Wednesday, one week earlier[1]

Industrial Production

Data are issued mid-month for the previous month

Capacity Utilization, Manufacturing, Mining, Utilities, and Materials

Selected Interest Rates

Data are issued mid-month for the previous month

Data are issued third working day of month for previous month

Consumer Installment Credit

Data are issued mid month for second month previous

FEDERAL HOME LOAN BANK BOARD

Thrift Institution Activity

Data are issued during last five working days of the month for previous month

DEPARTMENT OF HOUSING AND URBAN DEVELOPMENT

Yields on FHA Insured New Home 30 Year Mortgages   22   21   21   22   22   20   23   22   22   23   24   22

Data are as of the first of the month

Agency Indicators	Jan	Feb	Mar	Apr	May	June	July	Aug	Sept	Oct	Nov	Dec
DEPARTMENT OF THE TREASURY Treasury Statement (The Monthly "Budget¹)	23	24	21	21	21	20	22	21	22	22	24	19

Data are for previous month

¹When the release date falls on a holiday, the data are released the next workday.

Index